MIGHTY MATHS

SIXTH CLASS

MY PRACTICE BOOK

g GILL EDUCATION

MIGHTY MATHS

Contents

The *Mighty Maths* Sixth Class Practice Book

- Provides structured daily Maths practice for Sixth Class
- Aligns with the *Mighty Maths* programme and Sixth Class Pupil's Book
- Progresses with the Pupil's Book so that all questions are achievable for the children
- Covers all the Learning Outcomes of the new Primary Maths Curriculum
- Revisits all the Strands and Strand Units (especially on Mondays) so that children get frequent exposure to the more difficult Strands and Strand Units of the curriculum
- Provides daily practice in mental Maths and problem-solving skills
- Provides a weekly assessment each Friday
- Full of engaging, child-friendly and cognitively challenging activities.

Please note:

The authors of the *Mighty Maths* programme suggest that the Practice Book is used **a week behind** the Pupil's Book to allow time for the Strand to be covered and to consolidate learning.

Monday | Look Back

1. Round 6,745 to the nearest thousand.

   _____

2. Write the number that is 400 greater than 56,445. _____

3.
   ```
       4 5 1 9 2
     + 1 1 6 0 7
   ```
   _____

4.
   ```
       7 m 1 8 cm
     − 5 m 4 5 cm
   ```
   _____

5. What is the average of 3, 4 and 5? _____

6. $\frac{6}{9} = \frac{\square}{3}$

7. (a) $\frac{1}{3} + \frac{1}{4} =$ _____

   (b) $\frac{5}{6} − \frac{1}{3} =$ _____

   (c) $2\frac{3}{8} − 1\frac{1}{4} =$ _____

8. Name the shape.

   _____

9. What type of angle is the clock showing?

   _____

10. (a) $3\frac{1}{4}$ hours = _____ hours _____ minutes

    (b) Write 6:15 p.m. in the 24-hour format.

    _____

    (c) How many seconds are in 135 minutes?

    _____

Tuesday

1. Show 327,185 on the abacus.

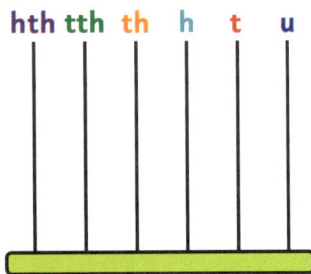

   hth tth th h t u

2. Round 575,436 to the nearest thousand.

   _____

3. Round 73.475 to one decimal place. _____

4. Find the values of the underlined digits.

   (a) 5,7̲36,192 _____

   (b) 1,854̲,381 _____

   (c) 2,859,1̲73 _____

   (d) 3,8̲43,596 _____

5. What is the largest number you can make using all of these digits? _____

   2   1   6   4   3   8

6. Model 5,374,218 on the notation board.

m	hth	tth	th	h	t	u

7. Write 25,835 in expanded form using figures.

   _____

   _____

8. Write 245,179 in expanded form using words.

   _____

   _____

   _____

9. Write the total amount of €5,000,000 + €300,000 + €10,000 + €4,000 + €200 + €60 + €7. €_____

10. (a) 5.3 > 5.27

    True ☐   False ☐

    (b) The value of 3 in 653,147 is 30.

    True ☐   False ☐

Wednesday

1. What is the value of the underlined digit in 3,562,1<u>8</u>7? _____

2. Write 46,927 in expanded form using figures.

   _____

   _____

3. Write 555,555 in expanded form using words.

   _____

   _____

   _____

4. Order from smallest to largest.

   939,645   973,422   946,485   928,746

   _____

5. Model 2,514,386 on the notation board.

m	hth	tth	th	h	t	u

6. Write three million, four hundred and twenty-one thousand, five hundred and seventeen in figures. _____

7. Write 245,179 in expanded form using words.

   _____

   _____

8. Round 253.324 to two decimal places.

   _____

9. Show 564,317 on the abacus.

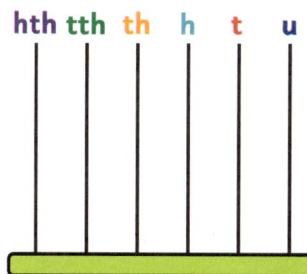

hth tth th h t u

10. Write the number 8,406 in words.

   _____

   _____

Thursday

1. What is the smallest number you can make using all of these digits?

   2   8   5   3   6   1   7

   _____

2. Use the Front-End Estimation strategy to round 553,828. _____

3. Find the value of the underlined digits in the number 3,<u>6</u>83,412.2<u>7</u>. _____

   _____

4. Model 4,365,183 on the notation board.

m	hth	tth	th	h	t	u

5. Order from largest to smallest.

   127,856   139,465   173,222   145,628

   _____

6. Round 365,251 to the nearest hundred.

   _____

7. What number is represented on the abacus?

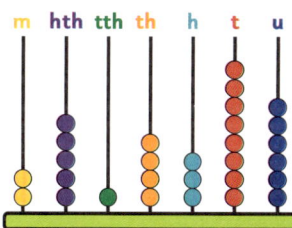

m hth tth th h t u

   _____

8. Write 134,280 in expanded form using figures.

   _____

   _____

9. Write the total of 1,000,000 + 200,000 + 30,000 + 7,000 + 700 + 40 + 8.

   _____

10. Round the number to complete the table.

Number	Nearest 10	Nearest 100	Nearest 1,000
19,126			

Monday | Look Back

1. What is the value of the underlined digit in the number 4<u>2</u>2,684? _____

2. Round €8.45 to one decimal place. €_____

3. (13,428 + 15,071) – 12,679 = _____

4.
```
    3 0 0 0 0 0
  – 1 5 8 2 6 4
  ─────────────
```

5. The marks obtained by five students are 70, 80, 75, 85 and 90. What is the average mark?

   _____

6. Find the area of the rectangle. _____ cm²

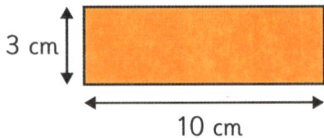

3 cm

10 cm

7. 30 mm = 0.3 m

   True ☐   False ☐

8. Name the shape. _____

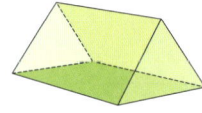

9. What type of angle is the clock showing?

   _____

10. Fill in the next 3 terms in the sequence below.

    12, 24, 36, _____, _____, _____

Tuesday

1. (a) 243 + 243 = _____

   (b) 53,618 + 17,331 = _____

2. (a) 21,478 – 7,349 = _____

   (b) (34,876 + 213,764) – 51,676 = _____

3.
```
    3 4 2 7 9 5
  + 5 8 3 8 6 7
  ─────────────

  ─────────────
```

4.
```
    4 2 3 7 9 5
  – 1 8 9 6 7 8
  ─────────────

  ─────────────
```

5.
```
    3 0 0 0 0 0
  – 2 6 5 3 6 1
  ─────────────

  ─────────────
```

6. The heights of three children, Clodagh, Shona and Billie-Rose, are 1.53 m, 1.57 m and 1.62 m. What is their total height combined?

   _____ m

7. Find the difference in height between the tallest and smallest child. _____

8. (a) 534,231 + 5,000 = _____

   (b) _____ – 442,653 = 313,630

9. (a) 897,346 – 50,000 = _____

   (b) 500,000 – _____ = 267,868

10. (a) 400,000 + 25,234 + 5,689 = _____

    (b) (543,011 + 257,154) – 311,874 =

       _____

Wednesday

1.
```
    2 5 6 3 8 9
  + 3 8 3 1 4 6
  _____
```

2.
```
    5 4 3 6 8 1
  - 4 8 2 7 9 4
  _____
```

3.
```
    5 0 0 0 0 0
  - 1 3 8 2 4 5
  _____
```

4. $8{,}278 + 2{,}543 - 7{,}618 =$ _____

5. Use the Front-End Estimation strategy to find a total estimate of:
$4{,}500 + 33 + 275 + 1{,}580 + 2{,}891.3 =$
_____

6. Éabha read 246 pages of her book. Cathal read 362 more pages than Éabha. How many pages did Cathal read?
_____

7. Use the Constant Difference strategy to find the difference between 12,000 and 9,534.
_____

8. On Wednesday, 235 people went to see the play. On Thursday, 455 attended and on Friday, 523 people attended. How many people saw the play over the 3 nights?
_____

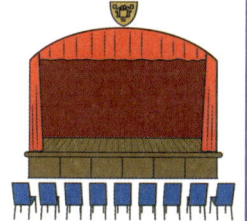

9. $123 + 333 =$ _____

10. (a) $57{,}941 - 21{,}800 =$ _____

(b) $400{,}000 -$ _____ $= 252{,}187$

Thursday

1. Use the Constant Difference strategy to subtract 224,681 from 400,000. _____

2. Use the Front-End Estimation strategy to find a total estimate of:
$53 + 418 + 35 + 113 + 27{,}685 =$ _____

3. (a) $53{,}135 + 24{,}678 =$ _____

(b) $341{,}982 + 438{,}179 =$ _____

4. Peter has €385 more than Danny in his bank account. If Peter has €880 in his bank account, how much does Danny have in his account? €_____

5. (a) Find the difference between 67,102 and 15,237. _____

(b) What must I add to 5,839 to get 20,000?
_____

6. (a) $812{,}387 - 75{,}748 =$ _____

(b) $(72{,}490 + 15{,}382) - (10{,}951 + 33{,}156) =$
_____

7.
```
    2 5 6 1 7 4
    1 2 3 1 4 6
  + 3 2 4 2 1 1
  _____
```

8.
```
    8 0 0 0 0 0
  -   6 4 0 5 7
  _____
```

9.
```
    5 4 3 4 2 9
  - 1 2 7 6 8 4
  _____
```

10. Raj and Ella are both reading the same book. The book has 346 pages. Raj has read 230 pages and Ella has read 185 pages. How many pages have they both left to read?

Raj: _____   Ella: _____

Monday | Look Back

1. Round the number 57.45 to the nearest tenth.

_____

2. Write the value of the underlined digit.

1,3̲87,381. _____

3. 500,000 − 235,681 = _____

4. 25 × 18 = _____

5. Find the area and perimeter of the rectangle.

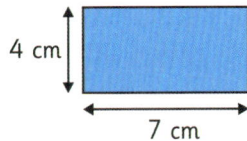

4 cm

7 cm

Area: _____ cm^2

Perimeter: _____ cm

6. (a) $\frac{4}{5} = \frac{\square}{10}$

(b) Write $\frac{18}{5}$ as a mixed number. _____

7. (a) 2 + 1.85 + 38.17 = _____

(b) Write $5\frac{1}{5}$ as a decimal number. _____

8. Name the shape.

_____

9. Draw an angle showing 55°.

10. The average of four numbers is 20. Three of the numbers are 15, 20 and 25. What is the fourth number? _____

Tuesday

1. (a) 40 × 10 = _____

(b) 4.19 × 10 = _____

2. Show the answer to 7.83 × 100 on the abacus below.

| th | h | t | u | $\frac{1}{10}$ | $\frac{1}{100}$ |

3. 375 × 18 = _____

4. Deirdre walked 16 km in a week. Jamie cycled five times as much as this the same week. How many km did Jamie cycle?

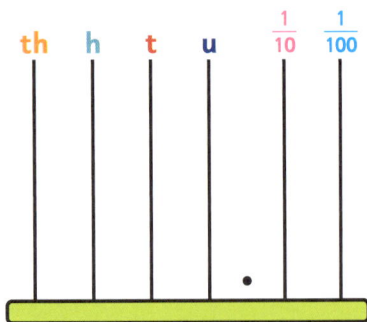

_____ km

5. (a) 256 × 32 = _____

(b) 6.35 × 100 = _____

6. A publisher prints 515 copies of a magazine. If each magazine has 96 pages, how many pages are printed in total?

_____

7. (a) 724 × 28 = _____

(b) 551 × 28 = _____

8. 6.3 × 100 = 63

True ☐   False ☐

9. Ayda is baking cookies for a bake sale. She plans to make 125 batches of cookies. Each batch contains 48 cookies. How many cookies will Ayda prepare in total?

_____

10. (a) 227 × 36 = _____

(b) 792 × 67 = _____

Wednesday

1. Leo's family is going on a road trip. They plan to drive 245 km each day for 5 days. How many km will they drive in total during the trip?

   _____ km

2. 288 × 19 = _____

3. A sports shop sells packs of sliotars. Each pack contains 24 sliotars, and the shop has received an order for 135 packs. How many sliotars have been ordered?

   _____

4. A concert hall has 345 seats. If a ticket costs €95, how much money will be made if every seat is sold?

   €_____

5. 215 × 26 = _____

6. 472 × 318 = _____

7. Marie is planting rows of flowers in her garden. She plants 27 rows, and each row has 36 flowers. How many flowers did Marie plant?

   _____

8. It costs 70c for one orange. How much would it cost to buy 16 oranges?

   €_____

9. It costs €2.50 to buy a bag of four oranges. How much would Darren save if he bought four bags of oranges instead of 16 loose oranges?

   €_____

10. 2.456 × 10 = _____

Thursday

1. 321.54 × 1,000 = _____

2. An art school buys 125 packs of coloured pencils. Each pack contains 48 coloured pencils. How many coloured pencils does the school purchase in total?

   _____

3. 2.8 × 100 = _____

4. 3 8 5
    × 2 8
    _____

    _____

5. A sports shop sells 175 basketballs, and each basketball costs €22. How much money will the shop make if all the basketballs are sold?

   €_____

6. 312 × 45 = _____

7.   1 8 4
    × 2 3 1
    _____

    _____

8. 45.6 × 100 = 0.456

   True ☐   False ☐

9. A landscaping company is planting trees in a park. They plant 430 trees in the first section of the park and 125 trees in the second section. If each tree costs €15, what is the total cost of all the trees?

   €_____

10. 1,836 × 217 = _____

Monday | Look Back

1. What is the value of the underlined digit in the number 518.$\underline{3}$4? _____

2. $356,187 + 288,982 - 415,342 =$

   _____

3.
   $$\begin{array}{r} 3\ 1\ 5 \\ \times\quad 2\ 6 \\ \hline \\ \hline \end{array}$$

4. $175 \div 5 =$ _____

5. (a) $315 \div 21 =$ _____

   (b) $18.2 \div 100 =$ _____

   (c) $810 \div 18 =$ _____

   (d) $840 \div$ _____ $= 70$

6. Write 6:24 p.m. in 24-hour format.

   88:88

7. An obtuse angle is greater than 90° and less than 180°.

   True ☐ False ☐

8. (a) How many vertices has a square-based pyramid? _____

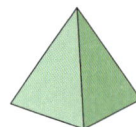

   (b) Do a square and a triangle tessellate? _____

9. $\frac{1}{2} + \frac{1}{4} =$ _____

10. A reflex angle is greater than 180° and less than 360°.

    True ☐ False ☐

Tuesday

1. The number 36 is both square and triangular.

   True ☐ False ☐

2. 1, 4, 9, 16, _____, _____, _____, _____

3. 2, 4, 8, 16, _____, _____, _____, _____

4. If the first term in a growing sequence is 3 and the difference between the consecutive terms is 0.25, what is the sixth term in the sequence?

5. What is the 4th triangular number? _____

6. The square root of 81 is 9.

   True ☐ False ☐

7. $3x = 18$

   $x =$ _____

8. If the first term in a growing sequence is 5 and the difference between each consecutive term is 20, what are the next five terms of the sequence?

9. (a) $\sqrt{81} =$ _____

   (b) $7 = \sqrt{\rule{2em}{0.4pt}}$

10. (a) $3^3 =$ _____

    (b) $4^2 =$ _____

    (c) $36 =$ ___^{2}

    (d) $25 = 3^2 +$ ___^{2}

Wednesday

1. $\frac{1}{2}, \frac{1}{3}, \frac{1}{4}, \frac{1}{5},$ _____, _____, _____

2. If the first term in a growing sequence is 15 and the difference between each consecutive term is 0.05, what is the 4th term of the sequence?

3. The number 16 is a square number.

   True ☐   False ☐

4. $\sqrt{49}$ = _____

5. 2^4 = _____

6. The 1st, 3rd and 5th terms in a sequence are 250, 750 and 1,250. What are the 2nd, 4th and 6th terms in the sequence?

   250, _____, 750, _____, 1,250, _____

7. $\sqrt{100} + 5^2$ = _____

8. Gavin is tracking how many pages he reads each night. He read 1 page on Monday, 2 on Tuesday, 4 on Wednesday and 8 on Thursday. If he continues with this pattern, how many pages will he read on Friday, Saturday and Sunday?

   Friday: _____

   Saturday: _____

   Sunday: _____

9. 4^3 = _____

10. 1, 3, 6, 10, _____, _____, _____

Thursday

1. $\sqrt{36}$ = _____

2. 2^5 = _____

3. 10, 100, 1,000, _____, _____, _____

4. Niamh started training for a run in January. When she started, she was able to run 3.5 km in 30 minutes. If she decreased her time by 15 seconds each month, how long would it take her to run the same distance in June? _____

5. −25, −20, −15, −10, _____, _____, _____

6. $3^3 + 13$ = _____

7. A plant grows 3 cm in one week, 6 cm in two weeks and 9 cm in three weeks. How many cm will it grow in the 4th, 5th and 6th weeks?

   3 cm, 6 cm, 9 cm, _____, _____, _____

8. 21 is the 6th triangular number.

   True ☐   False ☐

9. Draw the missing triangular numbers in the sequence.

10. 23 + 52 = _____

Monday | Look Back

1. $345 \div 23 =$ _____

2. (a) $176 \div 22 =$ _____

   (b) $132 \div 11 =$ _____

   (c) $144 \div 12 =$ _____

3. A cake stand holds 16 cupcakes. How many cake stands would you need for 640 cupcakes?

   _____

4. What is the difference between $-5°C$ and $5°C$?

   _____ °C

   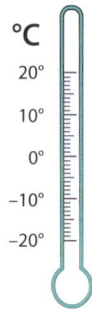

5. $7 + (-2) + 3 =$ ____

6. Colour $\frac{1}{12}$ of the grid blue. Colour $\frac{1}{6}$ of the grid yellow. Colour $\frac{1}{4}$ of the grid red.

7. $\dfrac{\boxed{}}{5} = \dfrac{4}{10}$

8. Write $\frac{17}{5}$ as a mixed number. _____

9. (a) $2\frac{5}{6} - 1\frac{4}{9} =$ _____

   (b) $2\frac{1}{2} + 3\frac{2}{4} =$ _____

10. Simplfy $\frac{18}{36}$. _____

Tuesday

1. 8 chairs have _____ legs

2. (a) $12.6 \div 6 =$ ____

   (b) $15.5 \div 5 =$ ____

   (c) $18.4 \div 4 =$ ____

3. James has 280 stickers. He wants to divide them equally into sticker albums. If each album holds 70 stickers, how many albums does he need?

   _____

4. There are 1,200 STEM kits to be shared equally among 30 classrooms. How many STEM kits will each classroom receive?

   _____

5. (a) $988 \div 52 =$ ____

   (b) $280 \div 7 =$ ____

6. A library has 2,563 books that they want to organise into shelves. Each shelf can hold 25 books. How many shelves will be completely filled? How many books be left over?

   Filled: _____   Remaining: _____

7. $4.574 \div 10 =$ ____

8. $5.74 \div 100 = 0.574$

   True ☐   False ☐

9. (a) $176 \div 22 =$ ____

   (b) $132 \div 12 =$ ____

   (c) $198 \div 18 =$ ____

10. A marathon event is transporting 4,812 participants to the starting line. If 36 participants can fit on each bus, how many buses will be needed to transport all the participants? _____

Wednesday

1. $1{,}272 \div 24 =$ _____

2. (a) $126.75 \div 100 =$ _____

   (b) $58.9 \div 10 =$ _____

   (c) $0.75 \div 10 =$ _____

3. (a) $240 \div 16 =$ _____

   (b) $198 \div 18 =$ _____

   (c) $144 \div 12 =$ _____

   (d) $117 \div 13 =$ _____

4. A concert hall has 768 seats. There are 24 equal rows of seats. How many seats are in each row? _____

5. $180 \div 100 = 1.8$

   True ☐   False ☐

6. A baker's tray holds 18 doughnuts. How many trays will it take to hold 2,232 doughnuts? _____

7. $72.8 \div 8 =$ _____

8. (a) $943 \div 41 =$ _____

   (b) $738 \div 41 =$ _____

   (c) $1{,}230 \div 30 =$ _____

   (d) $984 \div 41 =$ _____

9. Lynn is saving up for a car that costs €8,400. How many months will it take her to save for the car if she saves €525 every month?

   _____

10. $331{,}547 \div 1{,}000 =$ _____

Thursday

1. $221.54 \div 100 =$ _____

2. (a) $6{,}885 \div 27 =$ _____

   (b) $5{,}670 \div 30 =$ _____

   (c) $7{,}200 \div 40 =$ _____

   (d) $4{,}928 \div 32 =$ _____

3. Tennis balls are being packaged into boxes, with 28 balls in each box. How many boxes will 588 balls fill?

   _____

4. A shopkeeper has 832 sweets. He needs to fill 16 bags with equal amounts of sweets. How many sweets will be in each bag?

   _____

5. $648 \div 36 =$ _____

6. (a) $42.7 \div 7 =$ _____

   (b) $63.0 \div 9 =$ _____

   (c) $45.6 \div 8 =$ _____

   (d) $36.4 \div 7 =$ _____

7. $21.3 \div 3 = 0.71$

   True ☐   False ☐

8. A car travelled 832 km on 26 litres of fuel. Calculate the average number of km the car travelled per litre.

   _____ km

9. $48.6 \div 10 =$ _____

10. A company has ordered 893 chairs for an event, and they plan to set up 47 rows of chairs. If they arrange the chairs evenly, how many chairs will be in each row? _____

Monday | Look Back

1. Write the value of the underlined digit in the number 518.3̲4. _____

2. 356,187 + 288,982 − 415,342 = _____

3. A factory produces 315 toys every week. How many toys does the factory produce in 26 weeks?

   _____

4. (a) 175 ÷ 5 = _____

   (b) 243 ÷ 9 = _____

   (c) 186 ÷ 6 = _____

   (d) 264 ÷ 8 = _____

5. Write 9:24 p.m. in digital format.

   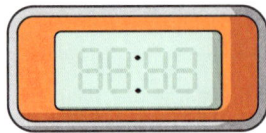

6. (a) 315 ÷ 21 = _____

   (b) 372 ÷ 12 = _____

   (c) 442 ÷ 26 = _____

   (d) 396 ÷ 18 = _____

7. An acute angle is greater than 90° and less than 180°.

   True ☐   False ☐

8. How many faces has a square-based pyramid?

   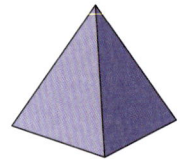

   _____

9. $\frac{1}{3} + \frac{2}{6}$ = _____

10. Do a square and a circle tessellate?

    Yes ☐   No ☐

Tuesday

1. −5 + 3 = _____

2. −10 − 7 = _____

3. Colour the thermometer to show −5°C.

   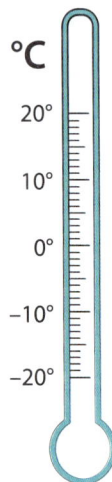

4. What is the difference between 12 and −5? _____

5. If I start on −3, add on 3 and subtract 4, what number do I land on? _____

6. −5 + (−2) = _____

7. Order the following temperatures from highest to lowest.

   12°C   −5°C   7°C   −2°C   8°C

   _____ _____ _____ _____ _____

8. In Donegal, the temperature at 6 a.m. is − 2°C. It increases by 1°C per hour for the next 4 hours. What is the temperature at 10 a.m.?

   _____ °C

9. Ellen has a bank balance of −€50 at the beginning of June. She receives €200 for her birthday in the middle of the month and spends €115 by the end of the month. What is Ellen's bank balance at the end of June?

   €_____

10. −5 + 8 = _____

Wednesday

1. Clodagh is three times the age of her sister, Shona. If Clodagh is 6, how old is Shona? Write a rule to describe this.

   _____

2. $-5 > -15$

   True ☐   False ☐

3. $-22 + 8 =$ _____

4. Order the temperatures on the number line.

   | −8°C | 7°C | 1°C | −5°C | −3°C | 4°C |

   −10°C   +10°C

5. Manchester United has played 6 games. They won 2 games, lost 2 games and drew 2 games. If a win is worth 2 points, a draw 1 point and a loss −2 points, how many points do they have altogether?

   _____

6. $-5 + (-7) =$ _____

7. A bank account has a balance of €100. On Monday, €20 is taken from the account. On Tuesday, €50 is added to it. On Wednesday, a fee of €15 is deducted. What is the account balance at the end of Wednesday?

   €_____

8. $3 + (-4) + (-2) =$ _____

9. −7, −15, −24, −34, ____, ____, ____, ____

10. If the first term in a sequence is 0.3 and each consecutive term is 0.4 greater, what is the fifth term of the sequence?

Thursday

1. (a) $-13 + 21 =$ _____

   (b) $9 - 30 =$ _____

   (c) $11 + (-5) =$ _____

2. Show −7°C on the thermometer.

   °C

   0°

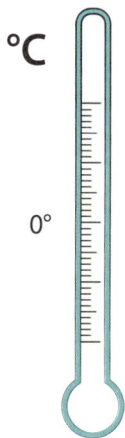

3. Temperatures dropped to −7°C overnight and rose to 3°C later that morning. What was the change in temperature?

   _____°C

4. Ring the coldest temperature.

   −5°C   −10°C   −7°C

5. $-10 + (-5) =$ _____

6. Ernie has €20 in his bank account. He owes his brother €30. Then he receives €25 for his birthday. If Ernie pays his brother back, how much will he have left? €_____

7. (a) $-6 + 6 =$ _____

   (b) $-12 - 4 =$ _____

   (c) $-2 + (-5) =$ _____

8. $3 + (-3) + (-7) =$ _____

9. The temperature inside a classroom is 18°C. The temperature outside is 22°C colder. What is the temperature outside? _____ °C

10. $5 - 8 =$ _____

1. (a) $5.632 \times 10 =$ _____

(b) $0.487 \times 10 =$ _____

(c) $13.9 \times 10 =$ _____

2. Alannah has a loyalty card which gives her a 15% discount on coffees. If the normal price for a coffee is €4.60, how much will Alannah pay after the discount?

€4.60

3. (a) $700,000 - 374,599 =$ _____

(b) $850,000 - 429,721 =$ _____

(c) $600,000 - 315,842 =$ _____

4. (a) $324 \times 21 =$ _____

(b) $417 \times 16 =$ _____

(c) $289 \times 34 =$ _____

5. (a) $25 \times 18 =$ _____

(b) $36 \times 14 =$ _____

(c) $48 \times 17 =$ _____

6. (a) $150 \text{ mm} =$ _____ m

(b) $1,200 \text{ mm} =$ _____ m

(c) $75 \text{ mm} =$ _____ m

7. (a) $5 \times \frac{2}{3} =$ _____

(b) $6 \times \frac{3}{4} =$ _____

(c) $8 \times \frac{5}{6} =$ _____

8. How many faces does a triangular prism have?

_____

9. What type of angle is the clock showing?

_____

10. $5,032 \text{ g} =$ _____ kg

1. (a) $\frac{1}{4} = \frac{\square}{12}$

(b) $\frac{2}{5} = \frac{\square}{20}$

(c) $\frac{3}{8} = \frac{\square}{32}$

2. (a) $30 \div 90 =$ _____

(b) $25 \div 40 =$ _____

(c) $6 \div 16 =$ _____

3. Write $\frac{18}{8}$ as a mixed number. _____

4. Find $\frac{2}{3}$ of 24. _____

5. Write the following as mixed numbers.

(a) $17 \div 5 =$ _____

(b) $23 \div 4 =$ _____

(c) $29 \div 6 =$ _____

6. (a) $\frac{3}{8} + \frac{1}{4} =$ _____

(b) $\frac{5}{6} + \frac{1}{3} =$ _____

(c) $\frac{2}{5} + \frac{1}{10} =$ _____

7. (a) $1\frac{1}{2} + 2\frac{3}{4} =$ _____

(b) $3\frac{1}{3} + 1\frac{2}{3} =$ _____

(c) $2\frac{1}{5} + 4\frac{2}{5} =$ _____

8. $\frac{5}{8} > \frac{3}{4}$

True ☐   False ☐

9. $\frac{15}{4} + \frac{23}{12} =$ _____

10. Aimee has €75. She spends $\frac{2}{5}$ of her money on clothes and saves the rest. How much money does she save?

Wednesday

1. (a) $\frac{2}{3} + \frac{1}{9} =$ _____

   (b) $1\frac{2}{3} + 2\frac{2}{5} =$ _____

   (c) $2 - \frac{3}{7} =$ _____

2. Write $\frac{16}{5}$ as a mixed number. _____

3. Shade in $\frac{3}{4}$ of this shape.

4. A theatre has 936 seats. $\frac{2}{3}$ have people sitting in them. How many seats are vacant?

5. $\frac{6}{7} - \frac{1}{2} =$ _____

6. Write $2\frac{4}{9}$ as an improper fraction. _____

7. A baker makes 2,232 cupcakes. He sells $\frac{6}{8}$ of them in the morning. How many does he have left to sell in the afternoon?

   _____

8. (a) $\frac{3}{9} = \frac{1}{3}$

   True ☐   False ☐

   (b) $\frac{2}{8} = \frac{4}{24}$

   True ☐   False ☐

9. (a) $2\frac{2}{5} - 1\frac{3}{4} =$ _____

   (b) $2\frac{1}{3} - 1\frac{3}{4} =$ _____

   (c) $1\frac{1}{5} - \frac{2}{3} =$ _____

10. There are 72 pencils in the classroom. The teacher distributes $\frac{4}{6}$ of the pencils to pupils. How many pencils does the teacher have left?

    _____

Thursday

1. (a) $\frac{32}{3} - \frac{14}{5} =$ _____

   (b) $5\frac{2}{3} - \frac{14}{4} =$ _____

   (c) $1\frac{1}{2} - \frac{12}{16} =$ _____

2. There are 32 pupils in Cara's class. On Monday, $\frac{2}{8}$ of pupils were absent. How many pupils were in class that day? _____

3. Find $\frac{3}{8}$ of 40. _____

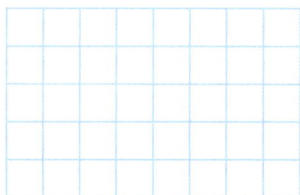

4. Order the fractions below from smallest to largest.

   $\frac{2}{3}$ $\frac{3}{4}$ $\frac{3}{6}$

   _____ , _____ , _____

5. Express the amount of pizza as an improper fraction.

   _____

6. (a) $\frac{3}{9} + \frac{2}{3} =$ _____

   (b) $\frac{15}{4} + 2\frac{3}{8} =$ _____

   (c) $\frac{10}{15} + \frac{6}{9} =$ _____

7. $3\frac{2}{5} - 2\frac{2}{3} =$ _____

8. Write $4\frac{5}{8}$ as an improper fraction. _____

9. Colour in $\frac{2}{5}$ of the chocolate bar.

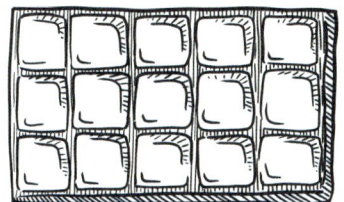

10. Levi has read $\frac{2}{3}$ of his book. If his book is 345 pages long, how many pages has he left to read? _____

Monday | Look Back

1. Simplify $4\frac{20}{25}$. _____

2. (a) $3\frac{1}{2} + 1\frac{6}{10} =$ _____

   (b) $\frac{15}{4} + 2\frac{3}{8} =$ _____

   (c) $\frac{20}{16} + \frac{24}{20} =$ _____

3. (a) $7\frac{1}{2} - 3\frac{3}{7} =$ _____

   (b) $2\frac{3}{4} - \frac{7}{3} =$ _____

   (c) $5\frac{3}{10} - \frac{3}{4} =$ _____

4. $2a + 8 = 20$. Find the value of a. _____

5. (a) Remi and Gia are going to the cinema. The film starts at 7:25 p.m. and ends at 10:05 p.m. How long is the film?

   _____

   (b) Write 7:25 p.m. in 24-hour format

   _____

   (c) How many minutes was the film?

   _____

6. Ger stops for a break after completing 55% of her cycle. If she stopped after 33 km, what was the total distance of the full cycle? _____ km

7. Draw an angle showing 135°.

8. (a) $7.16 - 3.514 =$ _____

   (b) $7 + 3.196 + 0.02 =$ _____

   (c) $17 - 2.514 + 3.77 =$ _____

9. Complete the next 3 terms of the sequence.

   1, 4, 9, 16, _____, _____, _____

10. The perimeter of a square is 44 cm. What is the area of the square?

    _____ cm²

Tuesday

1. (a) $3 \times \frac{3}{4} =$ _____

   (b) $\frac{4}{5} = \frac{\square}{40}$

2. (a) $\frac{3}{7} \times \frac{4}{5} =$ _____

   (b) $\frac{3}{5} + \frac{2}{6} =$ _____

3. Jane buys a book for $\frac{1}{3}$ of its original price. If she paid €9 for the book, what was the original price of the book?

   €_____

4. $5 \div \frac{1}{4} =$ _____

5. Simplify the ratio 12:18. _____

6. $3 \div \frac{3}{5} =$ _____

7. A sum of €600 is divided between three children in the ratio of 5:4:1. Tom received the largest amount and Anna received the smallest. How much money did Cara receive?

   €_____

8. $2\frac{1}{2} + 3\frac{2}{3} =$ _____

9. $5\frac{2}{3} - 4\frac{3}{5} =$ _____

10. Shade in $\frac{2}{3}$ of the shape.

Wednesday

1. There are 10 boys and 8 girls in a class. Write this as a ratio in its simplest form.

   _____

2. (a) $3 \times \frac{5}{9} =$ _____

   (b) $\frac{3}{9} \times \frac{5}{11} =$ _____

3. (a) $2\frac{2}{3} - 1\frac{3}{6} =$ _____

   (b) $5\frac{6}{10} - \frac{3}{4} =$ _____

   (c) $7\frac{4}{12} - 2\frac{2}{3} =$ _____

4. $6 \div \frac{2}{3} =$ _____

5. (a) Shade in $\frac{3}{7}$ of the shape.

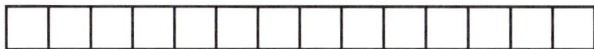

   (b) Find $\frac{5}{8}$ of 64. _____

   (c) $\frac{2}{5}$ is €36. Find the full amount. €_____

6. Sam has €36 left after spending $\frac{2}{3}$ of his money on clothes. How much money did he have to begin with?
   €_____

7. $\frac{8}{12} > \frac{2}{3}$

   True ☐   False ☐

8. A box of apples and oranges has a ratio of 2:3. If there are 18 apples, how many oranges are there?

9. A jug of milk has 250 ml left and is $\frac{1}{8}$ full. How much milk can the jug hold?
   _____ l

10. Haleem spends and saves his money in the ratio of 3:4. If he spends €21, how much did he have at first?

Thursday

1. How many thirds are there in 18? _____

2. (a) $12 \div \frac{2}{3} =$ _____

   (b) $20 \div \frac{4}{5} =$ _____

   (c) $15 \div \frac{5}{8} =$ _____

3. If $\frac{3}{7}$ is 9, what is the whole number? _____

4. (a) $\frac{5}{6} \times \frac{6}{7} =$ _____

   (b) $\frac{5}{6} \times 5 =$ _____

   (c) $\frac{3}{10} \times \frac{5}{6} =$ _____

5. Killian spends 30 minutes doing his Maths homework. This is $\frac{2}{5}$ of the amount of time it took to do all his homework. How long did he take to do all his homework?

6. (a) Write the correct symbol (>, < or =).

   $\frac{2}{7}$ ☐ $\frac{1}{3}$

   (b) Simplify $\frac{48}{60}$. _____

   (c) Write $\frac{19}{5}$ as a mixed number. _____

7. Alyna buys five chocolate bars. She shares $\frac{1}{3}$ of the chocolate equally among her friends and herself. How much chocolate does she have left? _____

8. $3 \div \frac{6}{8} =$ _____

9. Ian has €50 and Aoife has €150. What is the ratio of Aoife's money to Ian's money in the simplest terms? _____

10. Lisa bakes a cake. Her sister Maria eats $\frac{2}{8}$ of it and her brother David eats $\frac{1}{4}$. How much cake is left?

Monday | Look Back

1. $3.17 \times 1{,}000 =$ _____

2. $284 \times 27 =$ _____

3. $3{,}268 \div 19 =$ _____

4. $3a = 72 \div 6$.

   $a =$ _____

5. Find the area and perimeter of the rectangle.

   Area = _____ cm²

   Perimeter = _____ cm

   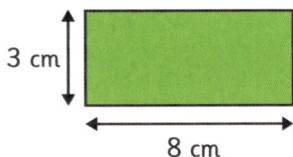
   3 cm
   8 cm

6. Jennie spent $\frac{7}{8}$ of her money on clothes. If she spent €84, how much did she have at first? €_____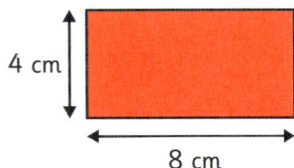

7. How many vertices does a cuboid have? _____

8. Find the surface area of this cube. _____ cm²

   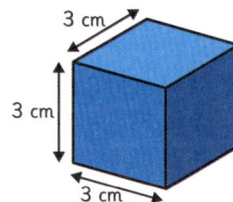

   3 cm
   3 cm
   3 cm

9. Draw an angle measuring 80°.

10. The ratio of hurleys to sliotars is 12:36. Write this in its lowest terms.

    _____

Tuesday

1. 2.7 cm = _____ mm

2. 185 mm = _____ m

3. Find the perimeter of the rectangle. _____ cm

   4 cm
   8 cm

4. How many metres are in 23 km? _____ m

5. 30 mm $+ 15$ cm $+ 1.2$ m = _____ mm

6. Find $\frac{3}{5}$ of a kilometre. _____ m

7. Calculate the perimeter of the shape. _____ cm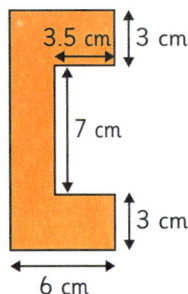
   3.5 cm 3 cm
   7 cm
   3 cm
   6 cm

8. Measure the line. _____ cm

9. Maya is 145 cm tall, Danii is 1.5 m tall and Calum is $1\frac{1}{4}$ m tall. What is the average height of the children?

10. Draw a shape that has a perimeter of 16 cm.

Wednesday

1. Calculate the perimeter of the shape.

   _____

   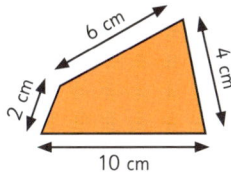

2. Draw a rectangle that has a height of 2 cm and a length of 5 cm.

3. Draw a line that measures 4.7 cm.

4. Find the difference between 275 cm and 0.83 m. _____ cm

5. 250 mm + 19 cm + 3.17 m = _____ mm

6. Use your ruler to measure the perimeter of this triangle.

   _____ cm

   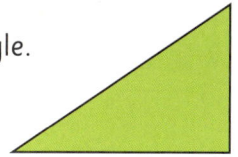

7. Saoirse is $\frac{2}{3}$ of the way through her bike ride. If she has cycled 56 km, how many kilometres has she left on her journey?

   _____ km

8. 2,436 m = _____ km

9. 28 cm < 280 mm

   True ☐   False ☐

10. Find $\frac{3}{4}$ of 64.8 km. _____ km

Thursday

1. Draw a line that measures 65 mm.

2. 150 mm is …

   15 cm ☐
   1.5 m ☐
   150 cm ☐

3. 8 mm = _____ cm

   _____ m

4. Write the correct symbol (>, < or =).

   1.75 m ☐ 175 mm

5. Calculate the perimeter of the shape.

   _____ cm

   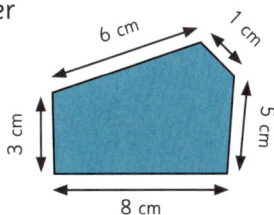

6. Finn is going on a 10 km run. He takes a break $\frac{3}{5}$ of the way through. How many metres does he have to run after his break?

   _____ m

7. 3.75 m + 226 cm − 450 mm = _____ cm

8. Raj's plant has grown to 0.63 m tall. How many cm would it need to grow to reach 1.5 m?

   _____ cm

9. A carpenter cuts a plank into three lengths: 3.35 m, 3.06 m and 2.8 m. Find the average length of the planks.

   _____ m

10. Draw a shape with a perimeter of 180 mm.

Monday | Look Back

1. Calculate the perimeter of the rectangle.

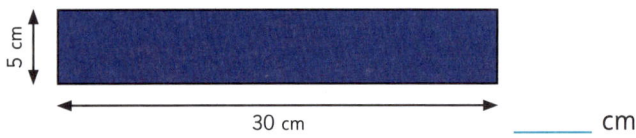

5 cm

30 cm

_____ cm

2. 217 × 56 = _____

3. 3b + 3 = 7 × 3

b = _____

4. 6,764 ÷ 38 = _____

5. Draw a line measuring 60 mm.

6. Write the correct symbol (>, < or =).

50 mm ☐ 0.5 m

7. How many vertices are there in a triangular prism? _____

8. Increase €64 by $\frac{3}{4}$. €_____

9. Convert 10:23 p.m. to 24-hour format.

_____

10:23

10. Triangular-based pyramids have 3 faces.

True ☐   False ☐

Tuesday

1. Find the area of this irregular shape.

_____ cm²

3 cm

5 cm

3 cm

8 cm

9 cm

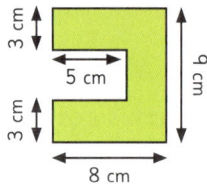

2. 60,000 m² = _____ hectares

3. Find the area of the triangle.

_____ cm²

4 cm

6 cm

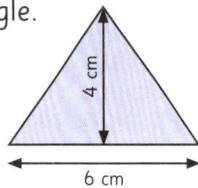

4. Find the area of the rectangle. _____ cm²

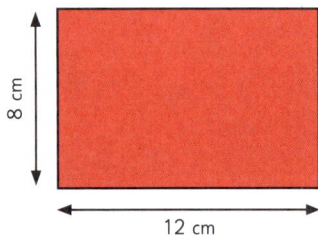

8 cm

12 cm

5. Find the surface area of the cuboid.

_____ cm²

3 cm

4 cm

6 cm

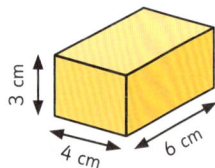

6. A map is drawn on a scale 1 cm : 50,000 cm. What length on the map represents 3 km?

_____ cm

7. How much would it cost to tile an 8 metre by 4 metre room if each tile is 1 m² and costs €12.50?

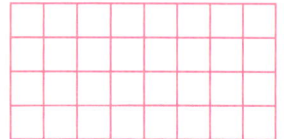

€_____

8. There are 5,000 m² in 5 hectares.

True ☐   False ☐

9. Sarah wants to plant a rectangular flower bed measuring 8 metres in length and 300 cm in width. What is the total area and perimeter of the flower bed?

Area: _____ m²

Perimeter: _____ m

10. A rectangular field has a length of 285 m and a width of 170 m. Find the area in hectares and km².

Hectares: _____

km²: _____

Wednesday

1. If the scale of a map is 1 cm to 10 m, what area does 1 cm² represent? _____ m²

2. What is the surface area of the triangular prism?

   _____ cm²

   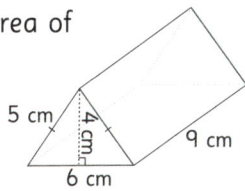

3. Find the area of the shape.

   _____ cm²

   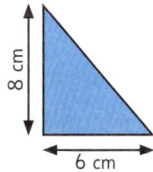

4. 17 hectares = _____ m²

5. What is the area of the triangle?

   _____ cm²

   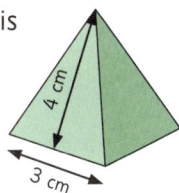

6. Find the area of a field with length 280 m and width 150 m in m² and hectares.

   m² = _____

   Hectares = _____

7. A rectangular floor measuring 6 metres by 5 metres is to be tiled. A mat measuring 3 metres by 2 metres covers part of the floor and does not need tiling. How much floor area needs to be tiled? _____

8. There are 12,000 m² in 12 hectares.

   True ☐   False ☐

9. Order the areas from smallest to largest.

   | 5 hectares | 3,000 m² | 25 km² |

   _____, _____, _____

10. Draw a shape with an area of 24 cm².

Thursday

1. _____ hectares = 62,000 m²

2. The area of a rectangular ice rink is 4,745 m². If the length of the rink is 146 m, what is the width? _____ m

3. Find the surface area of this square-based pyramid.

   _____ cm²

4. The area of a shape is always equal to its perimeter. Ring the correct answer.

   Always   Sometimes   Never

5. Draw an irregular shape with an area of 36 cm².

6. Find the perimeter of this irregular shape.

   _____ cm

   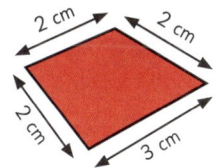

7. 15.35 hectares = _____ m²

8. Find the surface area of the cuboid.

   _____ cm²

   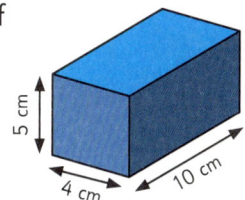

9. Find the area of a rectangle with a height of 13 cm and a length of 25 cm. _____ cm²

10. Find the surface area of the cube.

   _____ cm²

   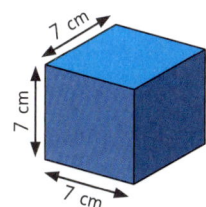

Monday | Look Back

1. (a) $2b = 18 + 2$

   $b =$ _____

   (b) $3x + 6 = 15$

   $x =$ _____

   (c) $3a = 3^2$

   $a =$ _____

2. Find the surface area of the cube.

   _____ cm²

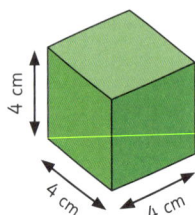

3. Convert 7:25 p.m. to 24-hour format.

4. (a) Round 85.567 to two decimal places.

   _____

   (b) Find the value of the underlined digit 134,678. _____

5. (a) $\frac{3}{5} = \frac{\square}{100} = 0.$____

   (b) Write $\frac{19}{3}$ as a mixed number. _____

   (c) Write $1\frac{7}{20}$ as a decimal number. _____

6.   2 4 4

   ×   3 6

   _____

   _____

7. Find the missing angle.

   _____ °

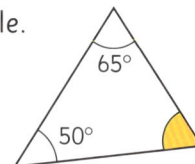

8. $6\frac{1}{2} - 2\frac{4}{7} =$ _____

9. The average of four numbers is 16. Three of the numbers are 15, 22 and 25. What is the fourth number?

   _____

10. (a) Increase 5,795 by 5,000. _____

   (b) $367 + 1,544 + 2,742 =$ _____

   (c) $(51,718 - 37,148) + 15,149 =$ _____

Tuesday

1. (a) Write $\frac{9}{100}$ as a decimal. _____

   (b) Write $\frac{22}{25}$ as a decimal. _____

   (c) Write $8\frac{9}{20}$ kg as a decimal. _____ kg

2. (a) Write 2.1 as a fraction. _____

   (b) Write 1.5 kg as a fraction. _____ kg

3. Order these from smallest to largest.

   $\frac{1}{2}$ 0.75 $\frac{2}{6}$ 0.4 $\frac{21}{100}$

   _____, _____, _____, _____, _____

4. Round 2.35 to one decimal place. _____

5. (a) $1.75 \text{ m} + 32 \text{ cm} + \frac{1}{5} \text{ m} =$ _____ m

   (b) $8.16 - 3.433 =$ _____

6. Write 6.572 in expanded decimal form.

   _____

7. (a) Round 8.734 to two decimal places. _____

   (b) Round 6.258 to one decimal place. _____

8. (a) 0.7 m = 7 cm

   True ☐   False ☐

   (b) 500 cm = 0.5 m

   True ☐   False ☐

9. Find the average of these heights:

   1.5 m, 145 cm and $1\frac{37}{100}$ m. _____ m

10. Write the next two terms of the sequence.

   3.033, 3.030, 3.027, _____, _____

Wednesday

1. 0.07 + 2.486 + 4.4 = _____

2. (a) Write the correct symbol (>, < or =).

   $2\frac{1}{2}$ ☐ 2.05

   (b) Round 1.873 to two decimal places. _____

   (c) $\frac{32}{50}$ = $\frac{\boxed{}}{100}$ = 0._____

3. Ben spends 0.15 of his money in one shop and 0.25 in another. If he has €18 left, how much did he have at first?

   €_____

4. (a) Round 85.675 to the nearest hundredth.

   _____

   (b) Write 0.009 as a fraction. _____

   (c) Write 1027 g as a decimal. _____ kg

5. 250 mm + 37 cm + 3.17 m = _____ m

6. $8\frac{3}{5}$ + 2.15 – 3.26 = _____

7. Write $2\frac{9}{20}$ as a decimal. _____

8. Order the numbers from largest to smallest:

   2.3 $1\frac{5}{10}$ 1.06 $2\frac{3}{4}$ 2.14

   _____, _____, _____, _____, _____

9. (a) 0.8 m > 8 cm

   True ☐   False ☐

   (b) $5\frac{1}{5}$ + 0.02 + 1.75 = _____

   (c) 11 – 2.507 = _____

10. Write 5.431 in expanded decimal fraction form. _____

Thursday

1. Write the correct symbol (>, < or =).

   (a) 4.7 ☐ $4\frac{7}{100}$

   (b) 1.246 ☐ $1\frac{246}{1000}$

   (c) $1\frac{1}{2}$ ☐ 1.2

   (d) 1.035 ☐ 1.35

2. (a) Round 7.564 to the nearest tenth. _____

   (b) Round 13.552 to two decimal places.

   _____

   (c) Round 3.4437 to three decimal places.

   _____

3. (a) Write 8.346 in decimal fraction form. _____

   (b) Write $\frac{11}{50}$ as a decimal. _____

4. Denise planned to cycle 24 km but got a puncture after cycling 0.25 of the journey. How far did she cycle?

   _____ km

5. 25 + 0.352 + 13.681 = _____

6. Write $22\frac{1}{4}$ in decimal form. _____

7. Write 3.4 as a mixed number in its lowest terms. _____

8. Tadgh has 3.75 m of ribbon. If he cuts off $\frac{3}{5}$ of the ribbon, how much does he have left?

   _____ m

9. (a) 7.26 – 3.431 = _____

   (b) 17 – 3.46 + 7.637 = _____

   (c) 25 + 0.362 – 11.165 = _____

   (d) $4\frac{1}{4}$ + 2.5 – $1\frac{1}{2}$ = _____

10. Arrange the following numbers from smallest to largest.

   1.2   1.25   1.03   1.21

   _____, _____, _____, _____

1. (a) $7{,}378 \div 34 =$ _____

   (b) $966 \div 42 =$ _____

   (c) $11.178 \div 100 =$ _____

2. 0.75 of children in a class have blue eyes. If 18 pupils have blue eyes, how many children are in the class in total?

   _____

3. What type of angle is shown on the clock?

   _____

4. Simplify $\frac{25}{30}$. _____

5. $1\frac{2}{5} + 3\frac{1}{4} =$ _____

6. Round 8.56 to one decimal place. _____

7. A hexagon and a square tessellate.

   True ☐   False ☐

8. (a) Decrease €120 by $\frac{3}{5}$. €_____

   (b) Increase 135 by $\frac{2}{5}$. _____

9. (a) $7^2 =$ _____

   (b) $2^2 + 5^2 =$ _____

   (c) $x^2 + 19 = 100$. Find the value of x. _____

10. $8 \div \frac{2}{3} =$ _____

Tuesday

1. Find 30% of 60. _____

2. $\frac{12}{20} = \dfrac{\Box}{100} =$ _____%

3. Write the correct symbol (>, < or =).

   (a) €300 ☐ 10% of €120

   (b) 20% of 355 ☐ 71

   (c) 55% of 200 ☐ 55

4. Using three different colours, shade in 32%, $\frac{1}{5}$ and 0.14 of the grid below.

5. Tia buys a box of eggs for €2.40 and sells them for €3.00. What percentage of profit does she make?

   _____

6. 75% of pupils in a school vote in favour of replacing the school uniform with a new tracksuit. If 156 pupils voted in favour, how many pupils are in the school altogether?

   _____

7. $85 \times 40\% =$ _____

8. $\frac{1}{8} = 8\%$

   True ☐   False ☐

9. Ring the largest number.

   $\frac{2}{5}$ 25%   0.2

10. A phone that originally costs €728 is reduced by 25% in a sale. What is the new price of the phone?

    €_____

Wednesday

1. Write the correct symbol (>, < or =).

   (a) 0.15 ☐ $1\frac{3}{20}$

   (b) $\frac{17}{25}$ ☐ 0.68

   (c) $12\frac{1}{2}\%$ ☐ 1.25

2. (a) Find 35% of 120. _____

   (b) 15% is €90. Find the full amount. €_____

   (c) 75% is €60. Find the full amount. €_____

3. Cal bought a bike for €250 and sold it for €230. What percentage of loss did he make?

   _____

4. Find $37\frac{1}{2}\%$ of 400. _____

5. $\frac{2}{5} = \frac{\boxed{}}{100} = $ _____%

6. 35% × 280 = _____

7. (a) Increase €90 by 25%. €_____

   (b) Decrease 72 by $12\frac{1}{2}\%$ _____

   (c) Find 15% of €420. €_____

8. Sadie spends 65% of her money on sports clothes. If she has €21 left, how much did she start with?

   €_____

9. An air fryer that originally cost €96 is reduced by $12\frac{1}{2}\%$ in a sale. What is the new selling price?

   €_____

10. Diarmuid bought a smartphone for €240. He sold it for €300. What percentage profit did he make on the smartphone?

    _____

Thursday

1. Using three different colours, shade in 12%, $\frac{1}{4}$ and 0.27 of the grid.

2. Find 55% of 240. _____

3. Cróia buys football boots for €80 and sells them for a 15% profit. How much does she sell them for?

   _____

4. Decrease 72 by 12.5%. _____

5. Ring the smallest number in the set.

   21%   0.12 $\frac{11}{100}$ $\frac{22}{100}$

6. (a) 78 × 28% = _____

   (b) 235 × 24% = _____

7. (a) $\frac{2}{4} = \frac{\boxed{}}{100} = 0.$_____ = _____%

   (b) $\frac{24}{\boxed{}} = 48\%$

8. (a) $12\frac{1}{2}\% = \frac{1}{8}$

   True ☐   False ☐

   (b) $33\frac{1}{3}\% = \frac{1}{3}$

   True ☐   False ☐

9. A video game originally cost €50 is now priced at €60. What is the percentage price increase on the game?

   _____

10. Maisie planted 30% of her flower seeds. If she planted 18 seeds, how many did she start with?

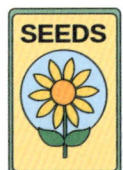

    _____

SEEDS

Monday · Look Back

1. × 5 = 45c

    = _____ c

2. (a) How many thirds are in 24? _____

   (b) Write $\frac{17}{4}$ as a decimal. _____

   (c) How many fifths are in 30? _____

3. (a) 700,000 – 564,379 = _____

   (b) 575,000 + 163,327 – 318,265 = _____

   (c) 200,000 – 19,543 + 46,279 = _____

4. A reflex angle is between 180° and 360°.
   True ☐   False ☐

5. Find the radius of a circle with a diameter of 7 cm. _____ cm

6. (a) $8^2 + 2^2 = $ _____

   (b) $7^2 + 3^2 = $ _____

   (c) $x^2 = 25 + 11$. Find the value of x. _____

7. $\frac{3}{5} \times \frac{2}{6} = $ _____

8. A film starts at 7:15 p.m. and finishes at 9:00 p.m. How long was the film?

   _____

9. (a) Find 35% of 140. _____

   (b) $12\frac{1}{2}$% is €72. Find the full amount. €_____

   (c) Find 17% of €255. €_____

10. 2 + 3.234 – 0.07 = _____

Tuesday

Use the information from the bar chart to answer the questions below.

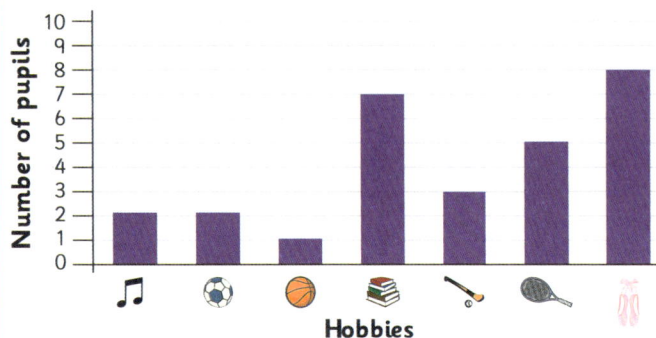

1. How many pupils were surveyed?

   _____

2. What is the most popular hobby?

   _____

3. What is the least popular hobby?

   _____

4. What percentage of pupils preferred reading?

   _____

5. Which hobbies had the same number of votes? _____

6. What fraction of pupils preferred music?

   _____

7. Complete the tally sheet using the two most popular hobbies surveyed.

Hobby	Tally

8. Find the average of the following lengths: 1.3 m, 135 cm and 1.13 m.

   _____ m

9. The average of four numbers is 15. Three of the numbers are 13, 16 and 17. Find the fourth number.

   _____

10. Over the months of November, December and January, Aisling reads 6, 10 and 5 books respectively. What was the average number of books she read each month?

   _____

Wednesday

Use the information about the Fifth and Sixth Class year groups from the bar chart to answer the questions.

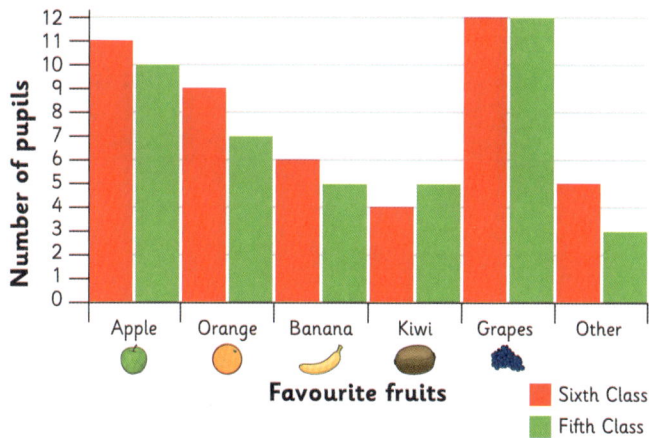

Favourite fruits

🟥 Sixth Class
🟩 Fifth Class

1. How many pupils were surveyed altogether? _____

2. How many pupils are in Fifth Class? _____

3. How many pupils are in Sixth Class? _____

4. What was the most popular fruit in Sixth Class? _____

5. What was the least popular fruit in Sixth Class? _____

6. Find the difference in votes between the most popular fruit in Fifth Class and the least popular fruit in Sixth Class. _____

7. Which fruit was equally popular in Fifth and Sixth Class? _____

8. Which two fruits did Fifth Class give the same number of votes? _____

9. What fraction of pupils in Fifth Class preferred apples? _____

10. Represent the information from the graph on the tally sheet below.

	Apple	Orange	Banana	Kiwi	Grapes	Other
Fifth Class						
Sixth Class						

Thursday

Use the information from the table to answer the questions below.

Type Sold	Mon	Tue	Wed	Thurs	Fri	Sat
Strawberry milkshake	17	18	19	25	30	11
Chocolate milkshake	20	22	26	22	36	14

1. Find the mean number of strawberry milkshakes sold, per day. _____

2. Find the mode of the number of chocolate milkshakes sold, per day. _____

3. Find the median of all of the sales figures shown in the table. _____

4. Find the range of chocolate milkshakes sold over the week. _____

5. Which milkshake is most popular? _____

6. Find the difference in sales between the two milkshakes on Wednesday. _____

7. Which day recorded the lowest number of sales? _____

8. Which day recorded the highest number of sales? _____

9. Find the mean of the two Friday sales figures. _____

10. Represent the information from the table on a tally sheet.

	Strawberry Milkshake Tally	Chocolate Milkshake Tally
Monday		
Tuesday		
Wednesday		
Thursday		
Friday		
Saturday		

Monday | Look Back

1. (a) $432 \times 24 =$ _____

   (b) $33.176 \times 100 =$ _____

2. (a) Find $\frac{3}{8}$ of 256. _____

   (b) $\frac{7}{8}$ is €49. Find the full amount. €_____

3. How many vertices has a square-based pyramid? _____

4. A pentagonal prism has 7 faces.

   True ☐   False ☐

5. (a) $7 \times 5 \times 4 \times 100 =$ _____

   (b) $3 \times 3 \times 3 \times 3 =$ _____

6. If $\frac{3}{5}$ is 18, what is the full amount? _____

7. (a) $5.7 \times 100 =$ _____

   (b) $35.186 \times 1,000 =$ _____

8. The radius of a circle is 4.5 cm. What is its diameter? _____ cm

9. 🍭🍭🍭🍭🍭 $= 5^2$

   🍭 $=$ _____

10. Ring the shape which is not a prism.

Tuesday

Use the information from the temperature graph to answer the questions below.

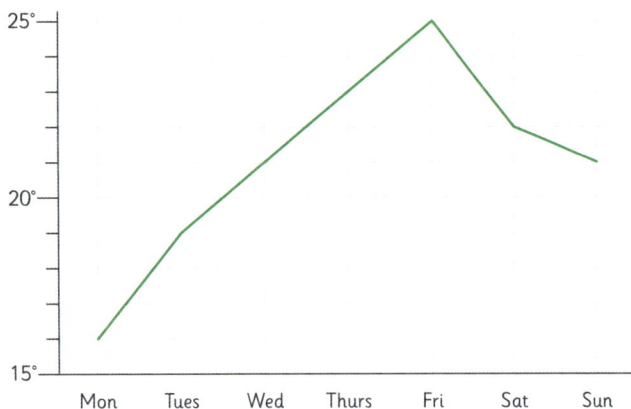

1. Find the mean temperature over the week.

   _____°C

2. Which day had the highest temperature?

   _____

3. Find the range in temperatures over the week.

   _____°C

4. Find the median temperature over the week.

   _____°C

5. Which day recorded the lowest temperature?

   _____

6. Between which two days is the greatest increase in temperature recorded? _____

7. What does the x-axis represent? _____

8. What was the mean temperature over the weekend? _____°C

9. What was the mean temperature from Monday to Friday? Round to the nearest whole number. _____°C

10. Represent the information from the temperature graph on a bar chart.

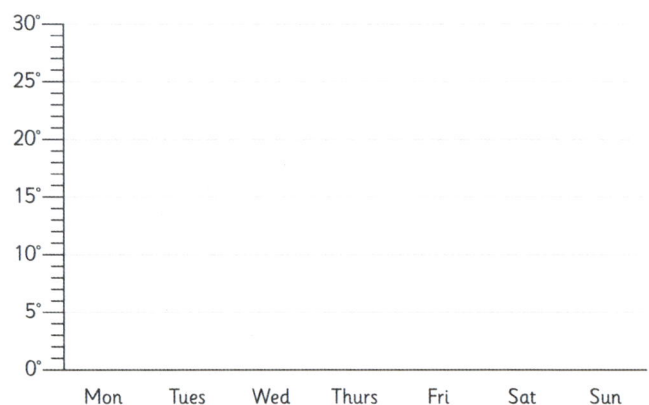

Wednesday

Use the information from the table below to help you answer the questions.

Fifth and Sixth Class held a readathon over 6 weeks.

Books Read		
Week	Fifth Class	Sixth Class
1	15	20
2	18	18
3	12	16
4	20	21
5	16	14
6	22	24

1. How many books did both classes read over the 6 weeks? _____

2. In which week did both classes read the same number of books? _____

3. Which week recorded the highest number of books read for Sixth Class? _____

4. Which week recorded the lowest number of books read for Fifth Class? _____

5. Find the average number of books read in Week 3 by both Fifth and Sixth Class. _____

6. What was the median number of books read by Sixth Class over the 6 weeks? _____

7. Express the number of books Fifth Class read to the number of books Sixth Class read in Week 1 as a decimal. _____

8. Use the Front-End estimation strategy to estimate how many books were read in total over the 6 weeks. _____

9. What was the median number of books read by Fifth Class over the 6 weeks? _____

10. What was the range of books read between Fifth and Sixth Class over the 6 weeks? _____

Thursday

This pie chart shows the favourite foods of 24 pupils in Sixth Class. Use the chart to help you answer the questions below.

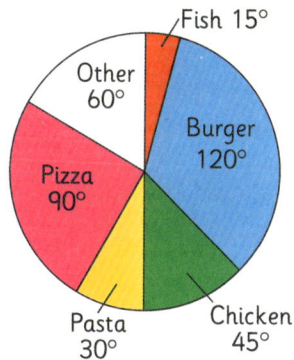

Fish 15°
Other 60°
Burger 120°
Pizza 90°
Pasta 30°
Chicken 45°

1. What percentage of pupils preferred pizza? _____

2. How many pupils liked chicken? _____

3. What fraction of pupils preferred pasta? _____

4. How many pupils prefer burgers? _____

5. Which food is the least popular? _____

6. Did any two foods receive the same number of votes? _____

7. Find the difference between the number of pupils who voted for pasta and the number who voted for pizza. _____

8. Write the popularity ratio of pasta to chicken to pizza in its simplest form. _____

9. Express the number of pupils who liked fish as a fraction to the number of pupils who liked burgers. _____

10. Draw a tally sheet to represent the number of students in each category from the pie chart.

Favourite Foods	Tally	Total
Fish		
Burger		
Chicken		
Pasta		
Pizza		
Other		

Monday Look Back

1. $5b = 21 + 4$

   $b =$ _____

2. Find the surface area of this cube.

   _____ cm^2

   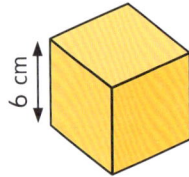

   6 cm

3. Convert 9:36 p.m. to 24-hour format. _____

4. Round 68.674 to two decimal places.

   _____

5. $\frac{3}{20} = \frac{\square}{100} = 0.$_____

6. $346 \times 27 =$ _____

7. Find the missing angle. _____°

   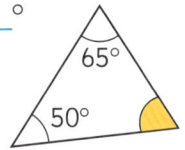

   65°
   50°

8. $8\frac{1}{2} - 3\frac{3}{8} =$ _____

9. The average of four numbers is 20. Three of the numbers are 32, 7 and 23. Find the fourth number.

   _____

10. Decrease 10,498 by 5,000. _____

Tuesday

1. Find the missing angle. _____°

   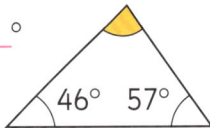

   46° 57°

2. Draw an angle measuring 70°.

3. A rectangle always has four right angles.

   True ☐   False ☐

4. Draw a triangle with a line of 5 cm, a line of 3 cm and angle measuring 60°.

5. Measure the angle. _____°

6. The diameter of a circle is 14 cm. What is the radius? _____ cm

7. Find the circumference of a circle with a radius of 3 cm. _____ cm

   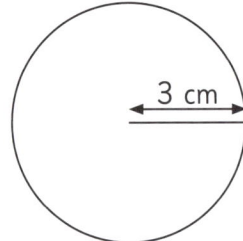

   3 cm

8. Find the missing angle. _____°

   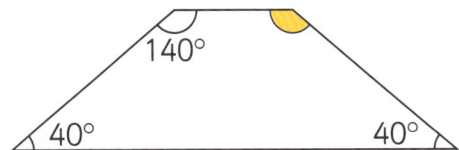

   140°
   40°   40°

9. Name this shape.

   _____

10. Ring the shape with 5 lines of symmetry.

Wednesday

1. The diameter of a circle is 15 cm. What is the radius? _____ cm

2. All angles in a triangle add up to 180°.

   True ☐   False ☐

3. Construct an angle measuring 120°.

4. The radius of a circle is 7.5 cm. What is the diameter? _____ cm

5. Find the missing angle.
   _____ °

   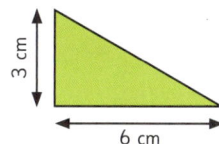
   90°   75°   95°

6. Find the circumference of a circle with a radius of 2 cm. _____ cm

7. The sum of the angles in an irregular pentagon is 540°. If one is 120°, what is the total of the other four angles? Ring the correct answer.

   210°   260°   420°   540°

8. Find the area of this triangle. _____ cm²

   3 cm   6 cm

9. Name this shape.

   _____

10. Use your protractor to measure the angle.

    _____ °

    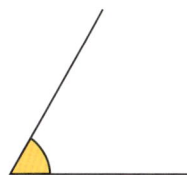

Thursday

1. The sum of the angles in a hexagon is 720°. If one angle measures 120°, what is the total of the other five angles? Ring the correct answer.

   540°   600°   260°   480°

2. Draw an angle measuring 75°.

3. Name this shape.

   _____

4. The diameter of a circle is 11 cm. What is the radius? _____ cm

5. Find 20% of 360°. _____ °

6. Find the circumference of a circle with a diameter of 5 cm. _____ cm

7. Find the missing angle.

   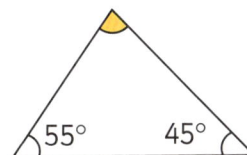
   55°   45°

8. All sides of a scalene triangle have different lengths.

   True ☐   False ☐

9. Find the perimeter of the triangle.

   _____ cm

   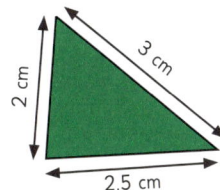
   2 cm   3 cm   2.5 cm

10. A triangle has a base of 8 cm and a height of 5 cm. What is its area? _____ cm²

    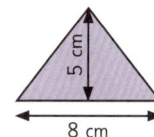
    5 cm   8 cm

Monday | Look Back

1. $7{,}378 \div 34 =$ _____

2. Simplify $\frac{25}{30}$. _____

3. In a class, 0.75 of pupils have green eyes. If 18 pupils have green eyes, how many pupils are in the class altogether? _____

4. $1\frac{2}{5} + 3\frac{1}{4} =$ _____

5. What is the measure of the angle shown on the clock?

_____

6. Round 8.56 to one decimal place.

_____

7. Draw a line measuring 50 mm.

8. Decrease €120 by $\frac{3}{5}$. €_____

9. $7^2 =$ _____

10. $8 \div \frac{2}{3} =$ _____

Tuesday

1. (a) Convert 3:15 p.m. to 24-hour format.

_____

(b) Convert 17:35 to 12-hour format.

_____

2. (a) 3 hrs 25 mins + 1 hr 55 mins =

_____ hrs _____ mins

(b) 2 hrs 36 mins − 1 hr 47 mins =

_____ hrs _____ mins

3. A film starts at 8:15 p.m. and finishes at 10:05 p.m. How long is the film?

_____

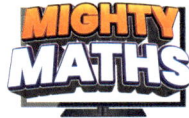

4. How many seconds are in one hour?

3,600 ☐

60 ☐

1,440 ☐

1,800 ☐

5. How many degrees are between each number on an analogue clock? _____ °

6. (a) 2 hrs 25 mins × 3 = _____ hrs _____ mins

(b) How many minutes are in $\frac{2}{5}$ of an hour?

_____

7. A game starts at 12:30 and finishes 2 hours and 10 minutes later. What time does it finish? _____

8. There are 72 hours in 3 full days.

True ☐   False ☐

9. Convert 3 hours 55 minutes to minutes.

_____

10. (a) A train leaves its station at 09:10 and travels for 2 hours 35 minutes. At what time will it reach its destination? _____

(b) If the train was delayed by 15 minutes, what time would it arrive? _____

Wednesday

1. Convert 255 minutes to hours and minutes.
   _____ hrs _____ mins

2. The school day starts at 08:50 and finishes at 14:30. How long is the school day?

   _____ hrs _____ mins

3. What is the measure of the angle shown on the clock?

   _____ °

4. Convert 7:32 p.m. to 24-hour format. _____

5. 3.5 hrs + 2 hrs 25 mins = _____ hrs _____ mins

6. 4.25 hrs − 2 $\frac{1}{4}$ hrs = _____ hrs _____ mins

7. It is 2 p.m. and Carol has a meeting at 16:45. How long does she have before her meeting starts? _____ hrs _____ mins

8. 3 hrs 20 mins × 2 = _____ hrs _____ mins

9. Write 22:18 in 12-hour format. _____

10. (a) Bobbi is uploading content to her YouTube channel. She uploads a video lasting 2 minutes 40 seconds. Convert this time to seconds.

    _____

    (b) Alan was recording content for his TikTok channel. If his video was 3 minutes 37 seconds, how many seconds did he record in total? _____

Thursday

1. (a) Convert 16:54 to 12-hour format.

   _____

   (b) Convert 2.51 p.m. to 24-hour format.

   _____

2. Emmet is watching a show on Netflix. The show lasts 45 minutes, and he watches $\frac{2}{3}$ of it before changing. How many minutes does he watch?

   _____

3. (a) 2 hrs 25 mins + 3 hrs 16 mins − 1 hr 27 mins = _____ hrs _____ mins

   (b) 3hrs 47 minutes − 2 hours 51 minutes =

   _____ hrs _____ mins

4. (a) 7 hrs 10 mins × 3 =

   _____ hrs _____ mins

   (b) 3 hrs 18 mins × 15 =

   _____ hrs _____ mins

5. How many hours are in 300 minutes? _____

6. A bus departs at 15:15 and arrives at its destination at 17:30. How long was its journey?

   _____ hrs _____ mins

7. Niall spends 25 minutes cooking every evening. How long does he spend cooking in a week? _____ hrs _____ mins

8. How many degrees are shown in the angle on the clock?

   _____ °

9. Kalli started studying at 3:45 p.m. and finished at 6:20 p.m. How long did she study for?

   2 hours 35 minutes ☐

   2 hours 45 minutes ☐

   2 hours 25 minutes ☐

   3 hours 15 minutes ☐

10. Shailesh gets up for work at 7:00 a.m. He spends 15 minutes getting ready and $\frac{1}{4}$ of an hour driving to work. At what time does Shailesh arrive at work? _____

Monday | Look Back

1. Find the surface area of this cuboid.

   _____cm^2

   (cuboid: 2 cm, 3 cm, 5 cm)

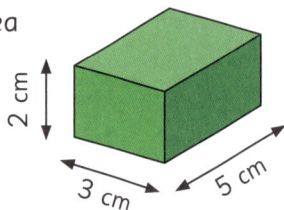

2. Convert 9:32 p.m. to 24-hour format.

   _____

3. Round 56.17 to one decimal place. _____

4. $\frac{3}{5} \times \frac{2}{8} =$ _____

5. 2.65 + 4.37 = _____

6. If $\frac{3}{8}$ of a number is 15, what is the number?

   _____

7. 🐠🐠🐠🐠🐠 + 15 = 25

   🐠 = _____

8. Write $\frac{29}{6}$ as a mixed number. _____

9. Aimee, Aoife and Brea share their sweets in the ratio 3:2:1. If there are 24 sweets altogether, how many sweets do they each get?

   Aimee _____

   Aoife _____

   Brea _____

10. Find 35% of 180. _____

Tuesday

1. A car travels a distance of 20 km in 30 minutes. How far will the car travel in an hour?

   _____ km

2. Bernard cycles at an average speed of 30 km/h. If he starts an 80 km cycle at 09:15, what time will he reach his destination?

   _____

3. Distance divided by time equals speed.

   True ☐   False ☐

4. Denise cycled for 40 minutes at an average speed of 27 km/h. How far did she cycle?

   _____ km

5. It takes Peadar 30 seconds to run 100 m. How long will it take him to run 750 m at the same pace?

   _____ mins _____ secs

6. A train travels at an average speed of 80 km/h. How long does it take to travel 300 km?

   _____ hrs _____ mins

7. (a) Convert 4:25 a.m. to 24-hour format.

   _____

   (b) How many minutes are in $\frac{5}{12}$ of an hour?

   _____

8. David travels 220.5 km in 3 hours. What is his average speed per hour?

   _____ km/h

9. During an ice-skating competition, Jackson skates 6 km in 12 minutes. What was his average speed per minute?

   _____ km/h

10. Order these times from earliest to latest.

    9:15 p.m.   2:00 a.m.   14:25   1:10 p.m.

    _____, _____, _____, _____

Wednesday

1. A train leaves a station at 09:05. It takes 255 minutes to reach its destination. At what time does it arrive at its destination? _____

2. Ciara walks 2.5 km in 30 minutes. How far will she walk in 2 hours? _____ km

3. Leon drives at an average speed of 12 km/h. How long will it take him to drive 30 km? _____ hrs _____ mins

4. Pat runs a 100 m sprint in 30 seconds. Liam runs the same sprint in $\frac{2}{5}$ of this time. What is Liam's speed per minute? _____

5. Convert 15:33 to 12-hour format.

_____

6. There are 40 minutes in $\frac{2}{3}$ of an hour.

True ☐   False ☐

7. A train travels 350 km in 2 hours. What is its average speed per hour? _____ km/h

8. Mary cycles at an average speed of 18 km/h. How long will it take her to cycle 54 km?

_____

9. Ger cycled 49 km in 1.75 hours. What was his average speed per hour? _____ km/h

10. A film starts at 16:40 and finishes at 20:10. How long is the film?

_____ hrs _____ mins

Thursday

1. (a) There are 36 minutes in $\frac{3}{5}$ of an hour.
   True ☐   False ☐

   (b) How many minutes are in $3\frac{1}{2}$ hours?

   _____

2. Write 17:27 in 12-hour format. _____

3. A car travels at an average speed of 84 km/h. How far will the car travel in 2.5 hours?

_____ km

4. A bus journey takes 42 minutes. If it leaves the station at 12:55, what time will it reach its destination? _____

5. Con rides his horse at an average speed of 14 km/h. How long will it take him to travel 35 km?

_____ hrs _____ mins

6. It takes Ian 40 seconds to sprint 100 m. How long will it take him to sprint 350 m?

_____ mins _____ secs

7. (a) Sajid travels 255 km in 2.5 hours. What is his average speed per hour?

_____ km/h

   (b) How far would Sajid travel in 5 hours?

   _____ km

8. How many minutes are there in $\frac{5}{6}$ of an hour?

_____

9. A plane flies at an average speed of 880 km/h. How far will it travel in 2.75 hours?

_____ km

10. Convert 2:37 p.m. to 24-hour format.

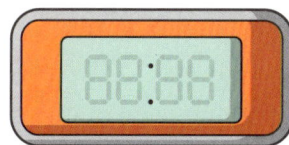

Monday | Look Back

1. 536 × 27 = _____

2. The diameter of a circle is 8 cm. Find the circumference.

   _____ cm

   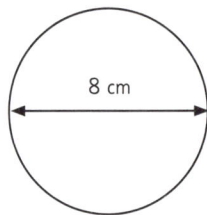
   8 cm

3. The perimeter of a square is 48 cm. Find the area.

   _____ cm²

4. How many metres are in 3.25 km?

   _____ m

5. Simplify $\frac{18}{24}$. _____

6. 3,268 ÷ 19 = _____

7. The radius of a circle is 4.5 cm. Find the diameter.

   _____ cm

8. $3^2 + 2^2$ = _____

9. $2\frac{1}{2} + 1\frac{7}{10}$ = _____

10. The average of four numbers is 20. Three of the numbers are 22, 19 and 21. Find the fourth number.

    _____

Tuesday

1. A painter applies 0.3 litres of paint to cover a section of the wall each time. If he paints 4 sections, how much paint does he use in total?

   _____ l

2. A library has 5 shelves, and each shelf has 2.7 metres of books. What is the total length of all the books on these shelves?

   _____ m

3. Aimee spent €4.75 on takeaway coffees each day in January. How much did she spend on takeaway coffee this month?

   €_____

   €4.75

4. Marie bought 4.5 m of material. Each metre cost €4.26. How much did she spend in total?

   €_____

5. 16.5 × 15 = _____

6. 51.3 × 27 = _____

7. 13 × 22.6 = _____

8. Tickets to the musical cost €55.25 each. Rebekah wants to buy 15 tickets. How much will she spend?

   €_____

9. 2.5 × 3.2 = 8

   True ☐   False ☐

10. What is the product of 2.3 and 1.6?

    3.68 ☐

    3.76 ☐

    3.86 ☐

    3.96 ☐

Wednesday

1. $17.5 \times 18 =$ _____

2. What number is 7.25 times greater than 18.62? _____

3. $23.15 \times 1.7 =$ _____

4. Paul has saved €556.54. Brea has saved 3.5 times as much. How much has Brea saved?

   €_____

5. $0.7 \times 0.4 = 2.8$

   True ☐   False ☐

6. $19.16 \times 0.24 =$ _____

7. Calculate the area of an ice-skating rink with a length of 59.9 m and a width of 28.8 m.

   _____ m²

8. $7 \times 0.17 =$ _____

9. Peter's car travels 16.5 km per litre of fuel. How far will 6.5 litres get him?

   _____ km

10. $19.267 \times 100 =$ _____

Thursday

1. $0.9 \times 0.9 = 0.81$

   True ☐   False ☐

2. $43.7 \times 0.26 =$ _____

3. Billy has 15.35 litres of petrol in his tank. He will need 5.7 times this amount to fill his tank. How much petrol can his tank hold?

   _____ l

4. $15.5 \times 25 =$ _____

5. (a) $352.9 \times 18 =$ _____

   (b) $17.673 \times 100 =$ _____

6. What number is 6.5 times greater than 28.17?

   _____

7. Tick the correct answer.

   $71.6 \times 4.7 =$

   336.77 ☐

   336.52 ☐

   335.77 ☐

   337.21 ☐

8. A factory consumes 16.673 litres of water every hour. How much water does it consume in 100 hours?

   _____ l

9. Natalia earns €16.26 an hour. How much does she earn after working 6.5 hours?

   €_____

10. $35.73 \times 0.26 =$ _____

1. A car travels at an average speed of 120 km/h. How far will it travel in 2.5 hours? _____ km

2. $2.5 \times 6.7 =$ _____

3. Round 667.235 to two decimal places.

_____

4. (a) $4 \div \frac{2}{3} =$ _____

(b) $\frac{2}{3} \times \frac{1}{5} =$ _____

(c) $5 \div \frac{1}{3} =$ _____

(d) $\frac{2}{6} \times \frac{1}{2} =$ _____

5. $7x = 49$

$x =$ _____

6. (a)
```
    2 2 3
  ×   2 7
  _____

  _____
```

(b)
```
    1 8 5
  ×   3 6
  _____

  _____
```

7. Convert 10:27 p.m. to 24-hour format.

8. All the angles in a quadrilateral add up to 360°.

True ☐   False ☐

9. (a) Find the area of a pitch that has a length of 25.5 m and a width of 8.7 m. _____ m²

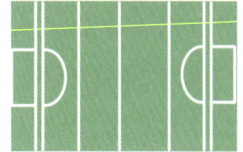

(b) What is the perimeter of the pitch? _____ m

10. (a) $1\frac{3}{5} + 3\frac{2}{3} =$ _____

(b) $2\frac{1}{4} + 1\frac{2}{8} =$ _____

(c) $3\frac{2}{3} - 1\frac{3}{6} =$ _____

(d) $5\frac{2}{5} - 3\frac{3}{30} =$ _____

1. $15 + (30 \times 2) \div 3 =$ _____

2. $82 + 2 \times 3 =$ _____

3. $(12 \times 6) \div 3^2 =$ _____

4. (a) $(30 + 5) \div 7 =$ _____

(b) $4 + 5 + 10 =$ _____

(c) $36 \div 3 \times 2 =$ _____

(d) $20 + 10 - 5 \times 3 =$ _____

5. (a) $(18 - 12) + 5 \times 4 =$ _____

(b) $(9 \times 5) \div (3 \times 5) =$ _____

(c) $6 \times (64 \div 8) =$ _____

(d) $5 \times 4 \times 3 \div 4 =$ _____

6. 🎒🎒 = 10

🎒 = _____

7. ⚽⚽⚽ × 4 = 36

⚽ = _____

8. Write an expression for an order of 3 pancakes, 2 waters and 1 orange juice.

_____

9. $3^2 + 4^2 =$ _____

10. $15 +$ 🎨 $+ 5 = 30$

🎨 = _____

Wednesday

1. 🍇🍇🍇🍇🍇 − 4 = 16

   🍇 = _____

2. $3 + a^2 = 28$

   $a =$ _____

3. (a) $(18 ÷ 3) × (15 ÷ 5) =$ _____

   (b) $(8 × 5) ÷ (4 × 2) =$ _____

   (c) $(46 + 14) × (15 × 2) =$ _____

   (d) $(81 − 17) × (4 × 2) =$ _____

4. $2^2 × 5^2 =$ _____

5. (a) $20 + 3 × 4 − 16 =$ _____

   (b) $10 × 5 ÷ (3 + 2) =$ _____

   (c) $56 − 5 × 11 =$ _____

6. $\frac{3}{5} x = 15$

   $x =$ _____

7. ✏️✏️✏️✏️ + 6 = 10 × 3

   ✏️ = _____

8. (a) $8 + (20 ÷ 5) × 6 =$ _____

   (b) $5 × (25 ÷ 5) + (9 × 2) =$ _____

   (c) $(84 ÷ 7) × 12 =$ _____

9. 🧽🧽🧽 + 5.5 = 14.5

   🧽 = _____

10. (a) Write an expression to show there are twice as many boys as girls in 6th class.

    _____

    (b) If there are 8 girls in the class, how many boys are in the class? _____

Thursday

1. $2 + c^2 = 83$

   $c =$ _____

2. $f^2 × 4 = 8^2$

   $f =$ _____

3. (a) $(27 − 8) − 5 =$ _____

   (b) $30 ÷ 5 × 3 =$ _____

   (c) $(72 ÷ 12) × 5 =$ _____

4. ▮▮▮▮▮▮ × 3 = 54

   ▮ = _____

5. Write an equation for this problem:
   A bookstore has 25 books on a shelf. They receive a new shipment of 5 boxes, each with 7 books. After selling 8 books, how many books are now on the shelf?

   _____

6. $\frac{2}{7} y = 14$

   $y =$ _____

7. $3 + 4 × 3 = 21$

   True ☐   False ☐

8. (a) $3 × 5 + 2 − 6 =$ _____

   (b) $17 + 56 ÷ 8 =$ _____

9. Write and solve an equation for this problem: Julie has €45. She is starting a book club and buys 5 books for €7 each. How much money does she have left?

   _____

10. (a) $5 × 3 × 2 ÷ 6 =$ _____

    (b) $6 + 6 × 6 ÷ 6 =$ _____

    (c) $5 + 5 × 5 ÷ 5 =$ _____

1. Find the surface-area of the cube.

   _____ cm²

   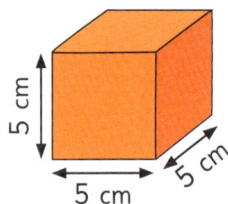
   5 cm | 5 cm | 5 cm

2. The radius of a circle is 11.7 cm. Find the diameter. _____ cm

3. All angles in a triangle add up to 180°.

   True ☐   False ☐

4. (a) 12 + 10 × 2 = _____

   (b) 7 + 7 × 7 = _____

   (c) (8 × 12) ÷ (4 × 4) = _____

5. What number is 5.6 times greater than 3.7?

   _____

6.
   ```
     5 0 0 0 0 0
   – 2 7 8 1 8 6
   ```

7. The radius of a circle is 4 cm. Find the circumference. _____ cm

8. (a) $3\frac{2}{5} - 2\frac{3}{4} =$ _____

   (b) $1\frac{2}{5} + 2\frac{2}{4} =$ _____

   (c) $7 \div \frac{1}{4} =$ _____

9. Find the average of the following numbers: 18, 12, 16 and 14. _____

10. (a) Increase 48 by $\frac{3}{8}$. _____

    (b) Decrease 30 by $\frac{5}{6}$. _____

    (c) Reduce 15 by $\frac{2}{5}$. _____

Tuesday

1. The bill in a restaurant is €85.70. VAT of 13.5% still needs to be added. To the nearest cent, what is the total cost of the bill?

   €_____

2. A smartphone costs €837, and this includes 23% VAT. How much VAT, to the nearest cent, is charged on the phone?

   €_____

3. Which is better value?

   45c ☐   €2.40 ☐

4. Which is better value?

   €2.50 ☐   €10.00 ☐

5. Sally wants to buy a hairdryer. It costs €178 before VAT at 23%. What is the total cost?

   €_____

6. Jean paid her hairdresser €50 for styling her hair. This included 13.5% VAT. To the nearest cent, how much VAT was charged?

   €_____

7. Which is better value?

   500 g €0.80 ☐   1.5 kg €2.70 ☐

8. A shop sells a 12 pack of markers for €4.80 and an 18 pack for €5.40. Which is better value for money?

   €_____

9. A painter charges €40 per hour. How much will it cost for 4 hours' work if he still has to add VAT at 13.5%.

   €_____

10. VAT of 23% is added to a dress costing €95. What is the total cost of the dress?

    €_____

Wednesday

1. 500 g of carrots costs €1.35. How much would 1.5 kg of carrots cost?

   €_____

2. Ami bought a TV for €545 plus VAT at 23%. How much did she pay in total? €_____

3. Celene paid €320 for two new tyres. This included VAT at 23%. To the nearest cent, how much VAT did she pay? €_____

4. Which is better value?

   2.5 kg of mince for €6 ☐

   4 kg of mince for €12 ☐

5. Which is better value?

   600 teabags for €24.00 ☐

   300 teabags for €18.00 ☐

6. Find 13.5% of €12.00. €_____

7. There is no VAT charged on children's clothing in Ireland.

   True ☐   False ☐

8. A carpenter charges €25 an hour before VAT. How much will he charge for 6 hours of work after 13.5% VAT is added?

   €_____

9. Dean's haircut cost €20 including VAT at 13.5%. To the nearest cent, how much VAT did he pay?

   €_____

10. Which is better value?

    1 kg of apples for €2.50 ☐

    2 kg of apples for €4 ☐

Thursday

1. In Ireland, hairdressers charge 13.5% VAT on their services.

   True ☐   False ☐

2. Which is better value?

   500 g = €1.50 ☐   Rice 1 kg = €4.50 ☐

3. A shops is offering a 20% discount on a €60 game. How much will the game cost after the discount?

   €_____

4. A tiler charges €30 an hour before VAT. How much will he charge for 5 hours of work after 13.5% VAT is added?

   €_____

5. Find 23% of €27. €_____

6. Find 13.5% of €18.00. €_____

7. Sarah wants to buy a pack of 5 cookies for €2.50 and Stephen wants to buy a pack of 8 cookies for €3.20. Which pack offers better value for money?

   _____

8. Petra wants to buy a lawnmower. It costs €120 before VAT at 23%. What is the total cost?

   €_____

9. Sergio buys a pair of runners for €115. This includes VAT at 23%. To the nearest cent, how much VAT was charged?

   €_____

10. Which is better value?

    €1.50 ☐   €5.00 ☐

1. Two angles in a triangle add up to 105°. Find the value of the third angle. _____ °

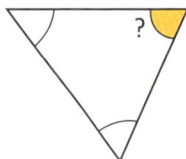

2. $0.015 \times 100 = 1.5$

   True ☐   False ☐

3. Balance the equation.

   $24 \div 8 = 9$ _____ 3

4. (a) Pio is six years older than Claudine. If Pio is 12, what age is Claudine?

   _____

   (b) How old will Claudine be when Pio is 60?

   _____

5. $x^2 + y^2 = 85$

   $x =$ _____

   $y =$ _____

6. (a) $525 \div 7 =$ _____

   (b) How many times can 5 be subtracted from 515? _____

   (c) $183 \div 3 =$ _____

7. (a) Increase 80 by 35%. _____

   (b) Decrease 90 by 30%. _____

   (c) Find 45% of 60. _____

8. $7 + 0.345 - 5.094 =$ _____

9.   1 2 . 3 4
    ×   5 6
    _____

    _____

10. Convert 17:17 to 12-hour format.

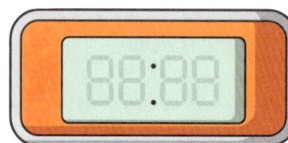

1. Olivia buys a dress for €40.00. She then sells it online for €60.00. What is her percentage profit? _____

2. Niall buys a shirt for €45 and sells it for 20% less. How much did he sell the shirt for?

   € _____

3. Sarah is travelling from Canada to Japan. The exchange rate is 1 CAD = 80 JPY. If she converts 500 CAD, how many JPY will she receive?

   _____

4. If a video game costs 60 USD and the exchange rate is 1 USD = 1.2 AUD, how much does the video game cost in AUD?

   _____

5. Calculate the simple interest on a loan of €6,000 with an APR of 10% over 6 years.

   € _____

6. Calculate the compound interest on a loan of €7,500 with an interest rate of 2% over 3 years. € _____

7. Which is better value for money?

   1 kg bag of rice for €4.80 ☐

   500 g bag of rice for €2.50 ☐

8. Which is better value?

   €2.50 ☐   €12.00 ☐

9. Ayda takes out a loan of €5,000. She doesn't make any repayments, so with simple interest it grows to €7,500 after 5 years. What is the APR charged on the loan? _____

10. Simple interest is calculated yearly as a percentage of the principal.

    True ☐   False ☐

Wednesday

1. Ring the correct answer. If the exchange rate between the USD and the EUR is 1 USD = 0.85 EUR, how much would you get if you exchanged 100 USD?

   €85   €115   €75   €100

2. Which is better value?

   70c ☐   €4.80 ☐

3. Calculate the compound interest on a loan of €2,000 with an APR of 5% over 3 years.

   €_____

4. If 1 GBP is equal to 1.35 USD, how much is 50 GBP worth in USD? _____

   $ £

5. A toy store buys a toy for €15 and sells it for €18. What is the percentage profit on each toy? _____

6. A 2-litre bottle of juice costs €2.40. A 1.5-litre bottle of the same juice costs €1.60. Which size is better value per litre? _____

7. Sheldon loans Penny €300 at a simple interest rate of 15% per annum. How much will she owe him after 3 years? €_____

8. A bike sold for €300 makes a 25% profit. What was the original cost price of the bike? €_____

9. If 16 markers cost €20.00, what is the cost of 1 marker? €_____

10. A customer buys a smartphone for €500 and later sells it for €400. What was the loss percentage? _____

Thursday

1. Compound interest is sometimes called interest on interest.

   True ☐   False ☐

2. If a pushchair is bought for €200 and sold for €250, what is the percentage of profit? _____

3. John has 100 euros and wants to convert it to US dollars at a rate of 1 EUR = 1.10 USD. How many US dollars will he have after the conversion? _____

4. Sarah sees a box of 20 chocolates for €12.50 and a box of 15 chocolates for €8.75 in her local shop. Which option is better value?

   _____

5. Which is better value?

   10 granola bars for €5.00 ☐

   20 granola bars for €9.00 ☐

6. Barry invests €2,000 at 6% interest per year, compounded annually. To the nearest cent, how much money will he have in total after 5 years? €_____

7. The exchange rate between the CAD and USD changes from 1 CAD = 0.75 USD to 1 CAD = 0.80 USD. How much more USD for 1 CAD would you get after the new rate? _____

8. Sean buys jeans for €80.00 and sells them for a €20 profit. What was the percentage profit on the jeans? _____

9. A sum of €1,500 is invested at a simple interest rate of 4% per year for 2 years. How much total interest is earned?

   €_____

10. A lady buys a dress for €1,200 and sells it for €1,500. Did she make a profit or a loss? How much?

    _____

Monday | Look Back

1. How many hectares are in 140,000 m²? _____

2. Order these numbers from smallest to largest:

   $\frac{7}{10}$, 1.7, 17%

   _____ , _____ , _____

3. Convert 10:49 p.m. to 24-hour format.

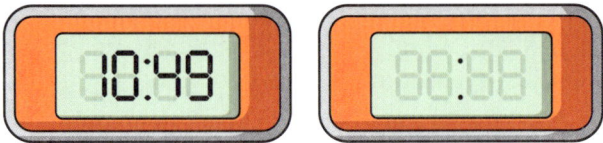

4. Calculate the area of a basketball court with a length of 25.4 m and a width of 14.3 m.

   _____ m²

5. Write 8.754 in expanded decimal form.

   _____

6. 10 + (4 × 4) ÷ 8 = _____

7. Which is better value?

 €33.00 ☐

 €24.00 ☐

8. VAT of 13% is added to a hairdryer that cost €239.00. How much does it cost after VAT?

   €_____

9. A loan of €6,000 is taken out for 3 years with compound interest at 2.5% per year. To the nearest cent, what is the total repayment due at the end of the 3 years, if no payments are made before that time? €_____

10. $15 + a + 20 = 9^2$

    a = _____

Tuesday

1. Selma cycled 36.4 km in 3.5 hours. What was her average speed per hour?

   _____ km/h

2. (a) 1.431 ÷ 0.27 = _____

   (b) 68.15 ÷ 47= _____

   (c) 569.5 ÷ 85= _____

3. (a) How many times is 6.7 contained in 8.71?

   _____

   (b) How many times can 1.5 be subtracted from 2.85?

   _____

4. 0.975 ÷ 7.5

   0.13 ☐

   1.3 ☐

   1.03 ☐

5. 10.101 ÷ 0.37 = _____

6. 0.25 ÷ 0.05 = 0.5

   True ☐   False ☐

7. 1.25 kg of flour costs €3.75. What is the cost per kg?

   €_____

8. (a) 7.506 ÷ 2.7 = _____

   (b) €94.83 ÷ €0.29 = _____

9. Ciara spent €6.30 downloading songs. She spent 90c on each song. How many songs did she download?

   _____

10. A container holds 11.25 litres of water. How many 0.75 litre bottles can be filled from one container?

    _____

Wednesday

1. (a) 1.248 ÷ 2.4 = _____

    (b) 34.5 ÷ 2.3 = _____

    (c) 28.05 ÷ 8.5 = _____

2. 3.75 ÷ 10 = 0.375

    True ☐   False ☐

3. How many planks measuring 0.64 m can be cut from a plank measuring 5.76 m?

    _____

4. Brea is paying off a holiday loan in instalments of €45.25. If the total cost of her loan is €859.75, how many instalments will she need to pay?

    _____

5. 1.950 ÷ 0.5 = _____

6. 0.036 ÷ 0.006 = _____

7. (a) 2.5 kg of oranges cost €6.00. What is the price per kg? €_____

    (b) How many kilograms of oranges would you get for €24? _____ kg

8. 332.8 ÷ 0.64 = _____

9. €45.90 is shared equally among a group of five. How much does each person receive?

    _____

10. 3.9 ÷ 0.78 = _____

Thursday

1. 8.1 ÷ 0.9 = 9

    True ☐   False ☐

2. (a) 0.658 ÷ 0.94 = _____

    (b) How many times is 0.26 contained in 9.204? _____

    (c) How many times can I subtract 6.4 from 8.256? _____

3. 2.090 ÷ 0.55 = _____

4. (a) How many times is 0.74 contained in 37.74? _____

    (b) How many times is 3.7 contained in 12.21? _____

    (c) Ciara spent €21.70 buying packets of stickers that cost €3.10 each. How many packets of stickers did she buy?

    _____

5. 5 ÷ 0.4 = _____

6. (a) 7.506 ÷ 2.7 = _____

    (b) How many times can I subtract 1.8 from 4.662? _____

7. (a) 5.248 ÷ 0.64 = _____

    (b) How many times will I find 0.17 in 57.12?

    _____

8. How many pieces of ribbon measuring 0.45 m can be cut from a 9 m long ribbon?

    _____

9. A cyclist rides a total distance of 75.6 km over several days. If they ride the same distance each day and ride 3.6 km per day, how many days did the cyclist ride? _____

10. Róisín ran 25 km in 2.5 hours. What was her average speed per hour?

    _____ km/h

Monday | Look Back

1. $x = 3$

   $2x + 5 = $ _____

2. What is the mode of the following numbers?

   3, 7, 3, 5, 9, 3, 2

   _____

3. The original price of a jersey was €60. There is 30% off it in the sale. What is the new sale price?

   € _____

4. Find the mean of the following numbers.

   5, 8, 12, 15, 20

   _____

5. If 3 notebooks cost €9, how much do 5 notebooks cost? € _____

6. Calculate the simple interest on €500 at 4% over 3 years. € _____

7. If Jane is twice as old as John and the sum of their ages is 36, how old is each person?

   Jane: _____

   John: _____

8. List the first 5 prime numbers.

   _____, _____, _____, _____, _____

9. A motorbike travels 120 km in 2 hours and 30 minutes. What is its average speed in km/h?

   _____ km/h

10. Ring the correct answer. What is the distance around a circle called?

    Diameter   Radius   Circumference   Area

Tuesday

Use the information on the spinner to answer the questions below.

1. What fraction of a full turn does the spinner need to make to land in the middle of the blue section?

   _____

2. If the spinner starts on red and does a full turn anticlockwise, which colour will it land on?

   _____

3. If the spinner lands on purple and rotates 180° clockwise, which colour will it land on?

   _____

4. How many degrees are the purple and blue sections in total? _____ °

5. How many degrees are in each section of the spinner? _____ °

6. What angle is shown on this clock?

   _____ °

   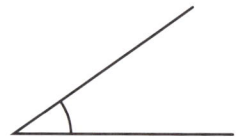

7. How many degrees are between 12 o'clock and 5 o'clock? _____ °

8. Use your protractor to measure the angle.

   _____ °

9. Draw an angle measuring 75°.

10. There are 270° in $\frac{3}{4}$ of a rotation.

    True ☐   False ☐

Wednesday

1. If you travel clockwise, how many degrees are there from north to southwest? _____ °

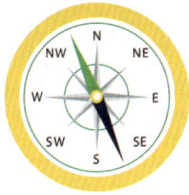

2. Ada travels anticlockwise from north-east to southwest. How many degrees does she travel? _____ °

3. How many degrees are there between the east point and the west point? _____ °

4. Paolo is facing towards the north. He turns to the east, then back to the northeast and finally back towards the east again. How many degrees did he rotate in total? _____ °

5. Darina is facing southwest. If she rotates by 135° anticlockwise, what direction is she facing? _____

6. A compass always points north.

   True ☐   False ☐

7. Eoghan is facing north and turns 135° clockwise. Which direction is he facing now?

   _____

8. Ring the correct answer. If you are facing south and want to turn to the west, how many degrees do you need to rotate?

   90°   180°   270°   360°

9. Measure the angle.

   _____ °

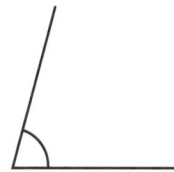

10. Draw an angle measuring 110°.

Thursday

1. What type of angle is shown on this clock?

   _____

2. How many degrees are shown in the angle on the clock above?

   _____ °

3. Find the measure of the reflex angle between the 9 and 1 on a clock face. _____ °

4. What time would it be if the minute hand in question 3 moved another 120° clockwise?

   _____

5. There are 150° in $\frac{2}{3}$ of a full rotation.

   True ☐   False ☐

6. The radius of a clock is 7 cm. Find the diameter. _____ cm

7. What is the circumference of the clock in question 6? _____ cm

8. What time would the clock show if the minute hand travelled $\frac{3}{4}$ of a full rotation in a clockwise direction?

   _____

9. Measure this angle. _____ °

10. Use a protractor to draw a 45° angle.

Monday | Look Back

1. Calculate the sum of 3,762 and 4,218.

   _____

2. What is the total area of the shape below?

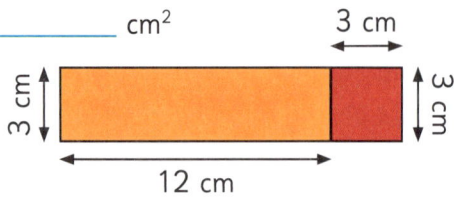

   _____ cm²

3. What is the place value of the digit 7 in the number 5,762?

   7   70   700   7,000

4. A gardener plants 64 rows of plants and each row has 128 plants. How many plants will the gardener plant in total?

   _____

5. 500,000 – 73,698 = _____

6. Round 4.68 to the nearest tenth. _____

7. A school library has 1,256 books. If a shelf can hold 32 books, how many shelves are needed to store all the books? _____

8. $3x = 3 \times 5$

   $x =$ _____

9. The ratio of boys to girls in a classroom is 3:2. If there are 24 boys, how many girls are there? _____

10. A painter mixes blue and yellow paint in a 1:4 ratio. If she uses 3 litres of blue paint, how much yellow paint does she need?

    _____ l

Tuesday

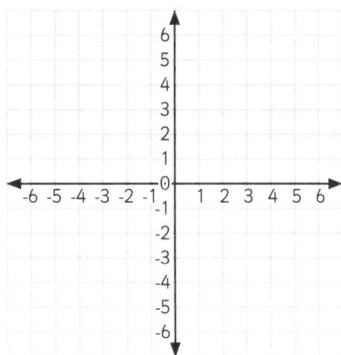

1. Plot the coordinates (2, 3) on the grid.

2. Plot the coordinates (–2, –3) and draw a line to join this point to (2, 3).

3. Draw a triangle on the grid with the coordinates: (–3, 1), (–5, 1), (–4, 4).

4. Draw a shape on the grid with the coordinates: (2, –2), (4, –2), (2, –4), (4, –4).

5. Name the shape you drew in question 4.

   _____

6. The angles in all quadrilaterals add up to 360°.

   True ☐   False ☐

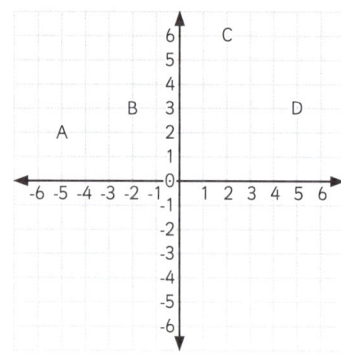

7. Find the coordinates of A and B on the grid.

8. Find the coordinates of C and D on the grid.

   A: _____
   B: _____
   C: _____
   D: _____

9. Plot the vertices of a triangle with the following coordinates: E (3, 4), F (1, –2), G (5, –2). What type of triangle is formed?

   _____

10. A vertex is:

    A vertical line ☐

    Where lines meet to form a point ☐

    A horizontal line ☐

    A V-shape ☐

Wednesday

1. Measure the angle. _____°

2. Latitude lines run from north to south.

   True ☐   False ☐

3. How many degrees are in a quadrilateral?

   _____°

4. Draw an angle measuring 80°.

5. What is the primary purpose of lines of longitude?

   To measure distances east and west ☐

   To measure distances north and south ☐

   To divide countries ☐

6. Draw a triangle using these coordinates: (–2, 1), (–5, 1), (–2, 5).

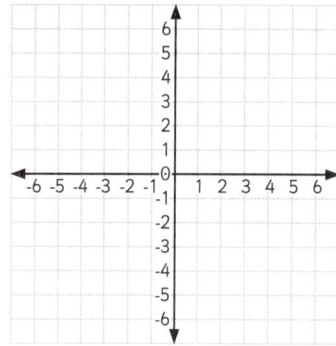

7. What type of triangle did you draw and how many degrees does it have?

   Triangle: _____   Degrees: _____

8. Draw a rectangle in the bottom right quadrant using coordinates of your choice.

9. Draw a scalene triangle in the bottom left quadrant using coordinates of your choice.

10. Given points D (2, 2), E (2, 6), F (6, 6), and G (6, 2), investigate whether these points form a rectangle. _____

Thursday

1. The Prime Meridian is located at 0° longitude.

   True ☐   False ☐

2. Draw an angle measuring 135°.

3. How many degrees are in $\frac{5}{6}$ of a full rotation?

   _____°

4. Measure the angle. _____°

5. You create a map of your neighbourhood where 1 cm represents 2 km. If, on the map, your house is 1.5 cm away from the school, how far is that in kilometres? _____ km

6. A map using a scale of 1:100,000 has a bridge measuring 2 cm in length. How long is the bridge in kilometres? _____ km

7. If a map key indicates that 1 cm represents 5 km, how many kilometres are represented by 4 cm? _____ km

8. On a map, the distance between two cities is 2.5 cm. If the scale is 1 cm = 20 km, what is the actual distance between the cities? _____ km

9. A classroom floor plan uses a scale of 1 cm = 1.5 m. If the classroom is 10 cm long on the plan, what is its actual length in metres?

   _____ m

10. A kitchen is represented as 3 cm wide and 4 cm long on the floor plan. If the scale is 1 cm = 0.5 m, what is the actual area of the kitchen in square metres? _____ m²

Monday | Look Back

1. Find the area of the triangle.

   _____ cm²

   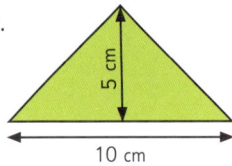

2. Calculate the circumference of the circle.

   _____ cm

   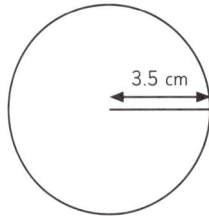

3. If a car travels at a speed of 60 km/h, how far will it travel in 2.5 hours?

   _____ km

4. A triangle has two angles measuring 35° and 75°. What is the third angle? _____°

5. Write 0.375 as a fraction, in its simplest form.

   _____

6. $5x + 12 = 32$. Find the value of x. _____

7. The ages of students in a class are 12, 13, 12, 14, 13 and 12. What is the mode of these ages? _____

8. A shop sells a €20 jersey with a 15% discount. What is the sale price of the jersey?

   €_____

9. Simplify $\frac{36}{48}$. _____

10. How many square metres are in 1.75 hectares?

    _____ m²

Tuesday

1. What is the probability of rolling a 3 on a standard six-sided dice?

   $\frac{1}{6}$ ☐ $\frac{1}{3}$ ☐ $\frac{1}{2}$ ☐ $\frac{1}{4}$ ☐

2. There are 10 juggling balls in a bag: 3 green, 4 yellow and 3 red. What is the probability of pulling out a green ball?

   _____

3. If you toss two coins at the same time, what is the probability of getting at least one tail?

   _____

4. A teacher has 7 boys and 5 girls in her class. If she randomly selects one student to answer a question, what is the probability that she picks a boy?

   _____

5. In a regular 52-card deck, what is the probability of drawing a heart?

   _____

6. A spinner is divided into 4 equal sections labelled A, B, C and D. What is the probability of the spinner landing on section C?

   _____

7. The probability of an event that is certain to happen is 0.

   True ☐   False ☐

8. If you flip a coin, what is the probability of it landing on heads?

   _____

9. The weather forecast reports a 70% chance of rain. What is the decimal probability that it will not rain?

   _____

10. If you roll 2 six-sided dice, what is the probability that the sum of the numbers on the top faces is 7?

    _____

1. A standard deck of cards has 52 cards. What is the probability of drawing an ace from the deck?

   _____

2. If you flip a coin, what is the percentage probability of it landing on tails?

   _____

3. A 50/50 chance means an even chance.

   True ☐   False ☐

4. There are 12 girls and 8 boys in a class. If one student is chosen at random, what is the probability that the student is a girl? _____

5. You have a bag with 4 red balls and 6 blue balls. If you pick a ball at random, what is the probability of it being a blue ball?

   $\frac{1}{2}$ ☐ $\frac{3}{5}$ ☐ $\frac{4}{5}$ ☐

6. How many possible outcomes are there when you flip two coins? _____

7. You have a bag with 2 apples, 3 bananas and 1 orange. If you pick a fruit at random, what is the probability of it being an apple?

   _____

8. You are playing chase with 8 of your friends. One of your friends is the chaser. What is the probability that you will be caught first?

   _____

9. A basketball team wins 60% of their games. If they played 10 games, how many games did they win? _____

10. A family has 2 boys and 3 girls. If one child is chosen at random, what is the percentage probability that the child is a girl? _____

1. A bag contains 5 red balls, 3 blue balls, and 2 green balls. If a ball is picked randomly from the bag, what is the probability that the ball is blue? Ring the correct answer.

   $\frac{1}{3}$ $\frac{3}{10}$ $\frac{1}{2}$ $\frac{2}{10}$

2. You draw a card from a standard deck of 52 cards. What is the probability of drawing a diamond?

   $\frac{1}{26}$ ☐ $\frac{1}{2}$ ☐ $\frac{1}{4}$ ☐

3. A spinner is divided into 8 equal sections: red, blue, green, yellow, pink, purple, orange and black. What is the percentage probability of landing on blue after spinning?

   _____

4. A jar contains 10 marbles: 4 black, 3 white, and 3 red. If you pick one marble randomly, what is the probability that it is not black?

   _____

5. The probability of an event that is certain to happen is 1.

   True ☐   False ☐

6. In a class of 20 students, 12 like chocolate ice cream and 8 like vanilla ice cream. If a student is chosen at random, what is the percentage probability that they like vanilla ice cream? _____

7. What is the decimal probability of rolling an even number on a standard six-sided dice?

   _____

8. What is the likelihood that the sum of two dice will be 9? _____

9. What is the probability of rolling at least one prime number when throwing two dice? _____

10. You flip a coin and roll a dice. What is the probability that the coin shows tails and the dice shows a number less than 4? _____

Monday | Look Back

1. If $2r + 3 = 15$, what is the value of r? _____

2. Convert $\frac{3}{4}$ to a decimal and a percentage.

   Decimal: _____ Percentage: _____

3. A car travels 60 km/h. How long will it take to travel 150 km?

   _____

4. Jamie invests €1,000 in a savings account that earns an annual simple interest rate of 5%. How much interest will he have earned after 3 years? €_____

5. What will be the total amount in Jamie's account after 3 years? €_____

6. A bag contains 3 red, 5 blue and 2 green marbles. If one marble is drawn at random, what is the probability that it is either red or blue? _____

7. At the moment, Bláithín is three times as old as her brother Seán. In 5 years, the sum of their ages will be 50. How old are Bláithín and Seán now? _____

8. The recipe for a fruit punch has a fruit juice to water ratio of 3:5. If you want to make 16 cups of punch, how many cups of fruit juice and how many cups of water will you need?

   Juice: _____ Water: _____

9. You have a monthly budget of €500. If you spend €150 on groceries, €100 on transportation and €80 on entertainment, how much money do you have left in your budget? €_____

10. $\frac{2}{3} \times \frac{4}{5} =$ _____

Tuesday

1. Convert 2.034 kg to grams. _____ g

2. Express 250 g as a fraction of 3 kg. _____

3. A melon weighs 4.5 kilograms. If 1.2 kilograms is eaten, how much melon is left?

   _____ kg

4. Jamie fills a bag with 750 g of apples. If she adds another 1.25 kg of apples to the bag, what will be the total weight of the bag in grams? _____ g

5. Sofia's backpack weighs 1.2 kg when it's empty. She adds the following items:

   Laptop: 2.5 kg

   Books: 1.8 kg

   Water bottle: 0.5 kg

   What is the total weight of her backpack with all the items included? _____ kg

6. 1.05 kg is the same as 1,005 g.

   True ☐ False ☐

7. Express 15 g as a percentage of 300 g. _____

8. It costs €13.00 to send a 20 kg parcel in Ireland. How much would it cost to send 15 parcels weighing 20 kg each?

   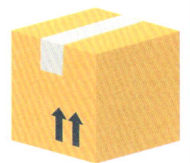

   €_____

9. A recipe for 12 cookies requires 150 g of chocolate chips. How many grams of chocolate chips would you need to make 36 cookies?

   _____ g

10. You have a bag of flour weighing 1.5 kg and use 25% for a recipe. How much flour is left in the bag?

    _____ kg

Wednesday

1. A recipe calls for 300 g of flour. If you want to double the recipe, how much flour will you need in total?

   _____ g

2. You need to carry 12 kg of books to school. If you can carry 5 kg at a time, how many trips will you need to make?

   _____

3. A 50/50 chance means an even chance.

   True ☐   False ☐

4. Express 30 g as a decimal fraction of 0.5 kg.

   _____

5. A puppy weighs 2 kg when it is born and gains 700 g each month. How much will it weigh after one year?

   _____ kg

6. A basketball weighs $\frac{3}{5}$ kg and a football weighs 450 g. What is the total weight of the two balls?

   _____ kg

7. A cake recipe requires 300 g of flour, 200 g of sugar and 50 g of butter. What is the total weight of the ingredients?

   _____ g

8. Using the ingredients from question 7, write the ratio of the amounts from the smallest measurement to the largest in its simplest form.

   _____

9. John catches a fish that weighs 2.8 kg. If he catches another fish that weighs 1.2 kg, what is the total weight of both fish?

   _____ kg

10. Convert 2.178 kg to grams. _____ g

Thursday

1. Children collect 3 kg of bottles one week, 2 kg the next week and 1.5 kg in the final week. How much did they collect in total?

   _____ kg

2. A dog weighs 12 kg. A cat weighs $\frac{1}{3}$ of the dog's weight. What is their total combined weight? _____ kg

3. Tom loses 2.5 kg after an illness. If his original weight was 78 kg, how much does he weigh now? _____ kg

4. 3,000 grams is equal to 3 kilograms.

   True ☐   False ☐

5. Sanita's backpack weighs 1.15 kg. If she adds a textbook that weighs 1.5 kg and a water bottle that weighs 0.5 kg, what will be the total weight of her backpack? _____ kg

6. Express 55 g as a fraction of 1.1 kg. _____

7. (a) Convert 3,001 g to kg. _____ kg

   (b) Convert 2.534 kg to grams. _____ g

   (c) Convert 4 $\frac{5}{8}$ kg to grams. _____ g

8. A rabbit weighs 2.2 kg, a guinea pig weighs 1,500 g and a tortoise weighs 3 kg. What is their combined total weight?

   _____ kg

9. A full suitcase weighed 30 kg. 10% of the weight was taken out. How much does it weigh now?

   _____ kg

10. If an elephant weighs 5,880 kg and a cheetah weighs 70 kg, how many cheetahs would weigh the same as one elephant?

   _____

Monday | Look Back

1. Round 12.721 to one decimal place. _____

2. Solve $763 \times 21 =$ _____

3. $200{,}000 - 176{,}453 =$ _____

4. Find the area and the perimeter of this shape.

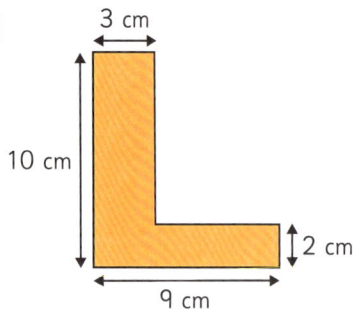

   3 cm

   10 cm

   2 cm

   9 cm

   Area: _____ cm²   Perimeter: _____ cm

5. $9^2 =$ _____

6. $\frac{1}{4} + \frac{2}{3} =$ _____

7. $3.8 \times 2.5 =$ _____

8. Write 3:15 p.m. in 24-hour format.

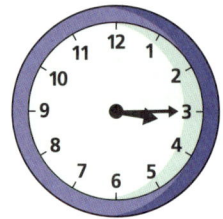

   _____

9. Simplify the ratio 12 : 6. _____

10. The average of 5 numbers is 10. Four of them are shown below. What is the 5th number?

    14   12   10   9   _____

Tuesday

1. Convert these measurements:

   (a) 180 ml = _____ l

   (b) 5,450 ml = _____ l

   (c) 6,300 ml = _____ l

2. What is 0.6 of 2 l? _____ l

3. Convert $\frac{3}{5}$ to a percentage. _____

4. Makayla and Maria each have a 200 ml cup of hot chocolate. Makayla drank $\frac{4}{5}$. Maria drank 75%. How many ml did they drink altogether? _____ ml

5. Complete the table.

	ml	Fractional Form	Decimal Form	Percentage
1.5 l juice	750	$\frac{1}{2}$		
1 l water	560			56%

6. Luke drank 35% of a full glass of milk. If he drank 210 ml, how much milk is in a full glass? _____ ml

7. Insert <, > or =.

   (a) 1,500 ml ☐ 1.5 l

   (b) 6.8 l ☐ 6,080 ml

   (c) $2\frac{1}{5}$ l ☐ 2,500 ml

8. Find the volume of this cube. _____ cm³

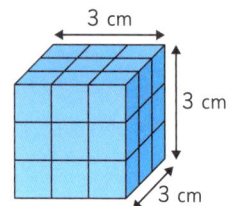

   3 cm

   3 cm

   3 cm

9. Find the volume of this cuboid. _____ cm³

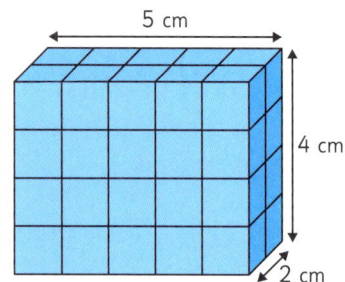

   5 cm

   4 cm

   2 cm

10. The volume of a cube is 216 cm³. Find the:

    (a) length _____ cm   (b) width _____ cm

    (c) height _____ cm

Wednesday

1. Find the volume of this shape. _____ cm³

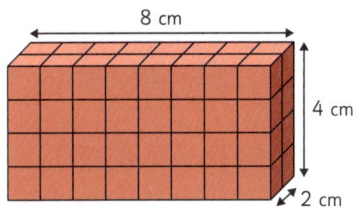
8 cm / 4 cm / 2 cm

2. Complete the table to show how much juice has been consumed from a 500 ml carton.

	ml	Fractional Form	Decimal Form	Percentage
Juice				72%

3. David drank $\frac{3}{5}$ of his smoothie. What percentage did he drink? _____

4. Colour 0.6 of the total capacity of this measuring jug.

5. Find 23% of 700 ml. _____ ml

6. The volume of cuboid is 24 cm³. If the length is 4 cm and the width is 2 cm, find the height.

_____ cm

7. $\frac{3}{\square}$ l = 0.3 l = _____ ml

8. Find the width of a cube with length 4 cm, height 4 cm and volume 64 cm³.

_____ cm

9. Ivy and Daisy were painting. Ivy used $\frac{11}{25}$ of 500 ml of green paint and Daisy used 0.35 of 500 ml of blue paint. How much more paint did Daisy use than Ivy?

_____ ml

10. 250 ml + 0.32 l = _____ ml

Thursday

1. Ring the correct answer. 0.4 of 400 ml =

160 ml   60 ml   206 ml

2. Olivia ordered a 350 ml smoothie. She drank 0.6 of it. How much was left? Complete the table.

ml	Fraction	Decimal	Percentage

3. 0.2 l + $\frac{5}{100}$ l + $\frac{1}{2}$ l + 132 ml = _____ ml

4. Find the volume of this cuboid.

_____ cm³

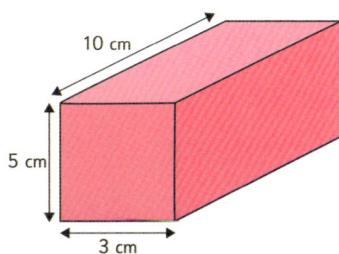
10 cm / 5 cm / 3 cm

5. The volume of a cuboid is 160 cm³. If the width is 5 cm and the length is 8 cm, what is the height? _____ cm

6. A recipe for fudge cake needs 450 ml of condensed milk. What percentage of a litre is 450 ml? _____

7. What fraction of this 600 ml graduated cylinder has been coloured in?

_____

8. Find 30% of 250 ml. _____ ml

9. 2.5 l × 0.3 l = _____ l

10. Ring the bucket with the greatest capacity.

725 ml   7.5 l $\frac{3}{4}$ l   75% l

Monday | Look Back

1. Round 13.652 to one decimal place. _____

2. 543,261 − 124,783 = _____

3. Find the volume of this cuboid. _____ cm²

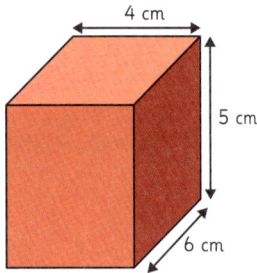

4. A concert started at 5:15 p.m. and ended at 6:45 p.m. How long did it last?

   _____ hr _____ mins

5. 468 ÷ 26 = _____

6. What is the 5th square number? _____

7. Solve 37.5 ÷ 2.5 = _____

8. If the exchange rate of € to GB£ is €1 to GB£0.84, how much GB£ would you get for €20? _____

9. Tick the better value option:

   1 bar of chocolate for €3.50 ☐

   5 bars of chocolate for €16 ☐

10. A car can travel 600 km on 50 l of fuel. How far could it travel on 75 l?

    _____ km

Tuesday

1. Which 3-D shape does this net make?

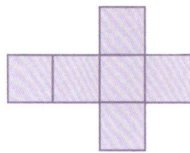

   _____

2. How many faces does a triangular prism have?

   _____

3. A cylinder is a prism.

   True ☐   False ☐

4. How many vertices does a square-based pyramid have? _____

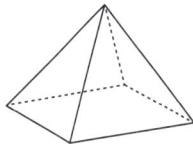

5. Name this shape.

   _____

6. Write another word for vertices.

   _____

7. Does this hexomino make a cube? _____

8. Draw a net of a cuboid.

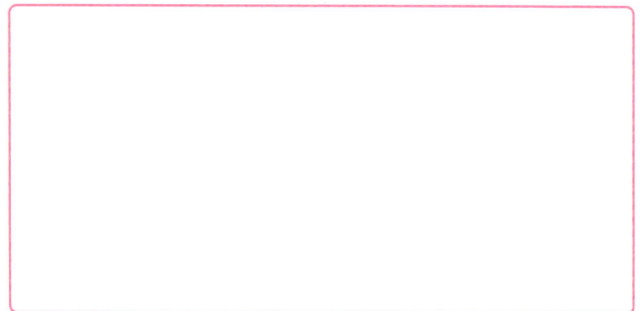

9. There are 9 coloured squares on each face of a Rubik's cube. How many coloured squares are there altogether? _____

10. What does 3-D stand for? _____

Wednesday

1. (a) Name this shape: _____

   (b) No. of edges: _____

   (c) No. of vertices: _____

   (d) No. of faces: _____

   (e) Type of faces: _____

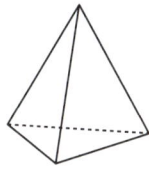

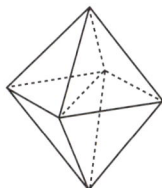

2. A tetrahedron is a triangular-based pyramid.

   True ☐   False ☐

3. Draw the net of a cylinder.

4. How many faces does a hexagonal prism have? _____

5. Name this shape.

_____

6. Which 3-D shape does this net make?

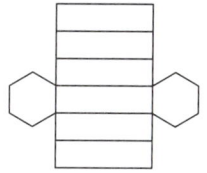

_____

7. Draw the top view of this shape.

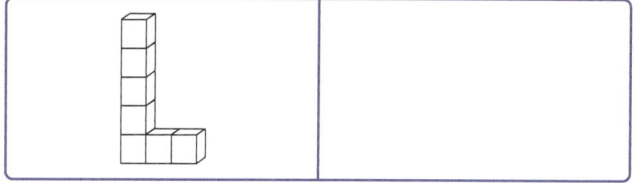

8. All prisms are platonic solids.

   True ☐   False ☐

9. How many vertices does a pentagonal prism have? _____

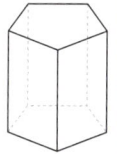

10. A solid is another word for a 3-D shape.

   True ☐   False ☐

Thursday

1. Draw the top view of this shape.

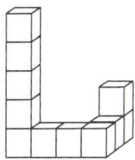

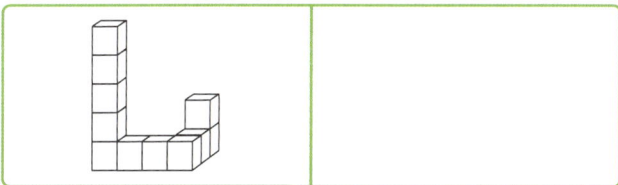

2. How many vertices does a tetrahedron have? _____

3. A cuboid has 6 rectangular faces.

   True ☐   False ☐

4. (a) Name this shape: _____

   (b) No. of edges: _____

   (c) No. of vertices: _____

   (d) No. of faces: _____

   (e) Type of faces: _____

5. I have 3 rectangular faces and 2 triangular faces. Which 3-D shape am I?

_____

6. Name this 3-D shape.

_____

7. Which 3-D shape does this net make?

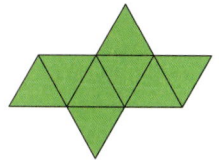

_____

8. Draw a net of a cube.

9. Ring the prisms.

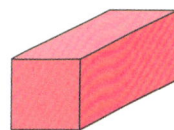

10. How many edges does a hexagonal prism have? _____

Monday | Look Back

1. Round 13,550 to the nearest hundred.

   _____

2. $56.34 \times 15 =$ _____

3. $215{,}734 + (200{,}000 - 176{,}453)$ _____

4. Convert 23:25 to 12-hour clock format and draw it on the clock face.

5. Find the surface area of this cuboid.

   _____ cm^2

   5 cm
   3 cm
   2 cm

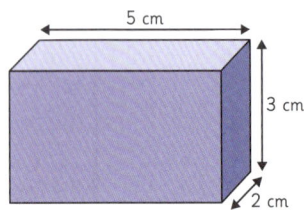

6. $\frac{2}{3} \times \frac{3}{5} =$ _____

7. How many thirds are in 9 circles? _____

8. The current season is _____.

9. Find the next 3 terms of the sequence.

   1, 3, 6, 10, _____, _____, _____

10. (a) If you start facing north and turn 45° clockwise, in which direction will you be facing? _____

    (b) If you then turned 135° anticlockwise, in which direction would you be facing?

    _____

    (c) How many degrees clockwise would you need to turn now to face north?

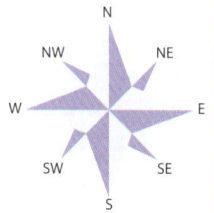

    _____

    N
    NW   NE
    W   E
    SW   SE
    S

Tuesday

Menu

Burger (b): €3.50

Chips (c): €1.60   Toastie (t): €7.20

Pizza (p): €10.00   Soup (s): €5.60

1. Use the menu to answer the following.

   (a) $2b + c =$ _____

   (b) $4p + 2t =$ _____

   (c) $s + t \times 3 =$ _____

2. Ring the prime numbers.

   2   5   7   9   15   23

3. ✗ the composite numbers.

   2   8   13   16   21

4. 2 is the only even prime number.

   True ☐   False ☐

5. 1 is neither prime nor composite.

   True ☐   False ☐

6. Find the highest common factor of 24 and 36. _____

7. Find the lowest common multiple of 8 and 4.

   _____

8. Draw the next term in this sequence.

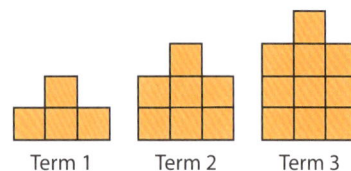

   Term 1   Term 2   Term 3

9. Write a rule for the terms in the sequence in question 8.

   _____

10. $95 + 23 = 72 + x$
    Find the value of x. _____

Wednesday

1. 5 and 7 are twin primes.

   True ☐   False ☐

2. Write the first 5 prime numbers.

   _____ _____ _____ _____ _____

3. Draw the next term in the sequence below:

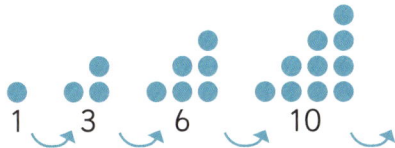

   1   3   6   10

4. What is the 6th triangular number? _____

5. Find the lowest common multiple of 5 and 6.

   _____

6. Find the highest common factor of 12 and 20. _____

7. Given $r = 3$, $y = 4$ and $b = 5.5$

   (a) Evaluate $2r + y \times b =$ _____

   (b) Evaluate $r^2 \times y^2 =$ _____

8. $2x + 3 = 18 - 1$.

   Find the value of x. _____

9. $y^2 + 3 = 21 \times 4$.

   Find the value of y. _____

10. Write an equation to represent the statement. A number multiplied by itself plus 3 is 67.

Thursday

1. Draw the next term in this sequence.

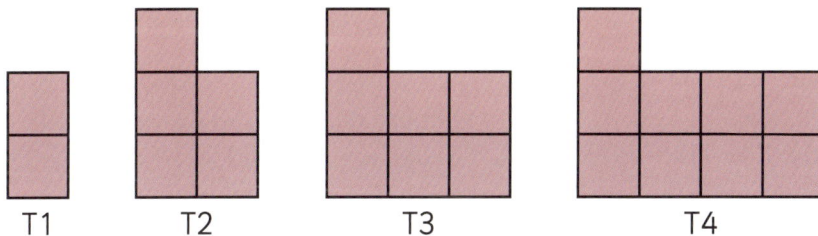

   T1   T2   T3   T4

2. Write a rule for the sequence in question 1. _____

3. Find the highest common factor of 15 and 60.

   _____

4. Find the lowest common multiple of 8 and 3.

   _____

5. 19 and 23 are cousin prime numbers.

   True ☐   False ☐

6. Write the next prime number:

   7   11   13   17   19   _____

7. Write an equation to represent the statement.

   A number minus 26 is 54. _____

8. $2x + 4 = 8$. Find the value of x. _____

9. Use the ice cream menu to evaluate the expression.

   $2s + 3m - c =$

   _____

   €2.50 s
   €3.75 c
   €3.00 m

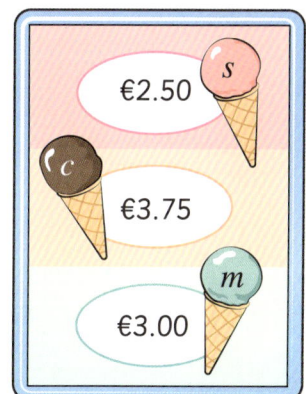

10. Write your own expression based on the ice cream and evaluate it.

    _____

Monday | Look Back

1. Round 65.237 to 2 decimal places. _____

2. Continue this pattern.

   1   4   9   16   _____   _____   _____

3. What is the next prime number after 19?

   _____

4. Find 75% of 200 ml. _____ ml

5. What is the probability of choosing a yellow cube from a bag of 4 blue cubes, 3 yellow cubes and 2 red cubes? _____

6. 7 and 9 are twin prime numbers.

   True ☐   False ☐

7. Find the average of 4.75, 1.15 and 5.35.

   _____

8. Ring the composite numbers:

   17   21   23   25   26   27   29   33

9. How many lines of symmetry does a hexagon have? _____

10. Calculate the missing angle.

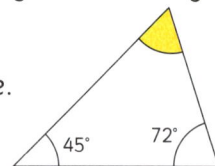

    _____ °

    45°   72°

Tuesday

1. Draw any lines of symmetry on the shapes below.

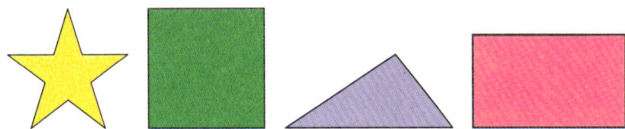

2. Ring the non-symmetrical letters.

   E   H   F   J   R   A

3. Draw the mirror image of this pattern.

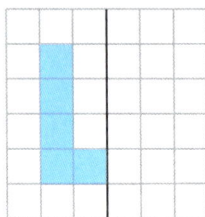

4. Write the coordinates of the vertices of the shape in Quadrant 3.

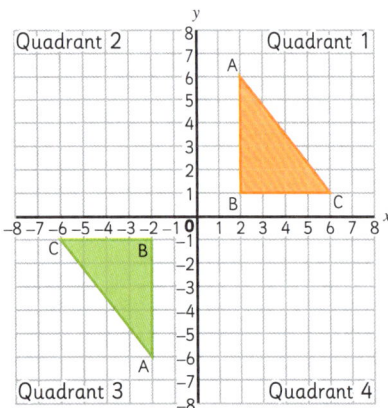

   A _____

   B _____

   C _____

   Quadrant 2   Quadrant 1

   Quadrant 3   Quadrant 4

5. Draw the mirror image of this shape.

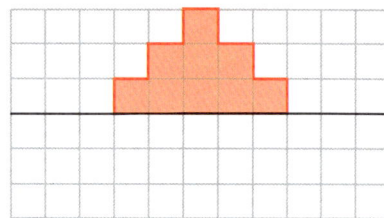

6. Write the coordinates of this shape if it was rotated 180° about the point (0,0).

   A' _____   B' _____

   C' _____

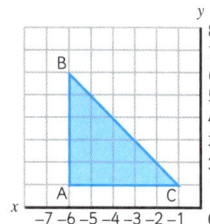

7. Ring the letters that have reflective symmetry.

   A   B   C   H   R   D   F

8. Draw the other half of this symmetrical shape.

9. Ring the correct answer. A rectangle has a rotational symmetry order of:

   2   4   1

10. What is the rotational symmetry order of this shape? _____

Wednesday

1. If this triangle was rotated 180° about the point (0,0), what would the coordinates be?

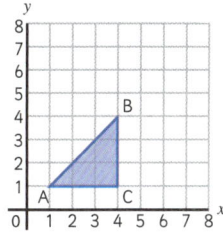

   A′ _____   B′ _____

   C′ _____

2. Draw the mirror image of this pattern.

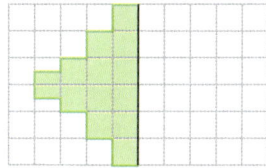

3. Ring the shapes that do not have reflective symmetry.

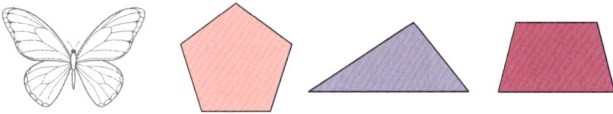

4. A nonagon has a rotational symmetry of 9.

   True ☐   False ☐

5. Draw the other half of this symmetrical shape.

6. Ring the correct answer. A regular heptagon has a rotational symmetry of:

   8   6   0   7

7. ✗ the symmetrical letters.

   D   H   L   S   C

8. Write the coordinates of the vertices of this shape.

   A _____   B _____

   C _____   D _____

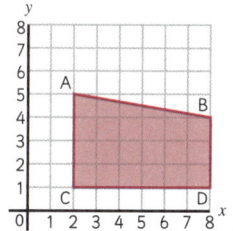

9. A parallelogram always has a line of symmetry.

   True ☐   False ☐

10. Reflect this shape through the diagonal line.

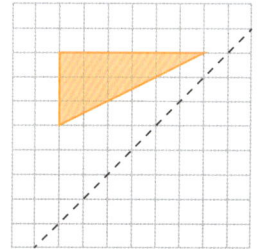

Thursday

1. Reflect this shape through the diagonal line of symmetry.

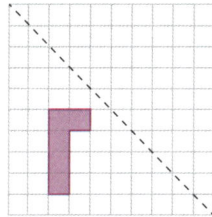

2. Rotate this shape 180° about (0,0) and label the coordinates of each vertex.

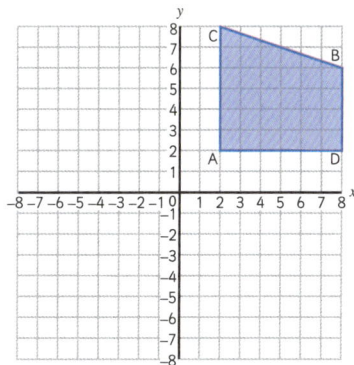

3. What is the order of rotational symmetry of this shape? _____

4. An equilateral triangle has a rotational symmetry order of 3.

   True ☐   False ☐

5. Ring the correct answer. The order of rotational symmetry for a regular decagon is:

   2   10   5   0

6. Draw any lines of symmetry in these shapes.

7. ✗ the letters with more than one line of symmetry.

   A   H   L   M   S   C   O   X

8. A square and a hexagon tessellate.

   True ☐   False ☐

9. Draw the mirror image of this pattern.

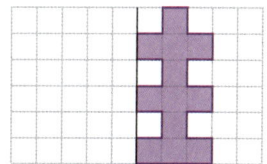

10. A parallelogram has 1 line of symmetry.

    True ☐   False ☐

Monday | Look Back

1. Find the surface area of this cuboid. _____ cm²

   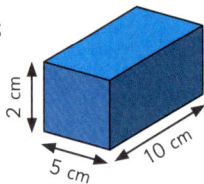

2. A point C (4, 2) is rotated 180° about the point (0, 0). What are the coordinates of the new point C′ after the rotation? _____

   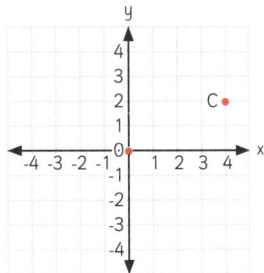

3. $\frac{5}{6} - \frac{1}{3} =$ _____

4. 3.17 × 2.5 = _____

5. Rollerblades that cost €40 are on sale for 25% off. What is the new sale price of the rollerblades? €_____

6. If the exchange rate is 1 USD $ = 0.85 EUR, how many euros will you receive for $150? €_____

7. A baker makes 240 cookies and packs them into boxes. If each box can hold 15 cookies, how many boxes does he pack? _____

8. $\frac{3}{5} > \frac{3}{4}$

   True ☐   False ☐

9. 23.5 – 7.42 = _____

10. A rectangle has a length of 12 cm and a width of 5 cm. What is the perimeter of the rectangle? _____ cm

Tuesday

1. A rectangle has a length of 5 cm and a width of 3 cm. If it is scaled up by a factor of 3, what are the new dimensions?
   Length: _____ cm   Width: _____ cm

2. A square garden has a side length of 2 m. If its side lengths are enlarged to twice their original length, what is the new perimeter of the garden? _____ m

3. What is the new area of the garden in question 2? _____ m²

4. A square has a side length of 10 cm. If it is scaled down by a factor of 0.5, what is the new area of the square? _____ cm²

5. A triangle has a base of 8 cm and a height of 5 cm. If it is scaled up by a factor of 2, what is the new area of the triangle? _____ cm²

6. A square has a side length of 10 cm. If it is scaled down by a factor of 0.25, what is the new area? _____ cm²

7. A cube has a volume of 27 cm³. If each of its sides is doubled, what is the new volume?
   _____ cm³

8. A triangle ABC is similar to triangle DEF. The sides of triangle ABC are 3 cm, 4 cm, and 5 cm. The sides of triangle DEF are 6 cm, 8 cm, and 10 cm. What is the scale factor from triangle ABC to triangle DEF? _____

9. Increase this irregular shape by a scale factor of 2 and then find the area. _____ cm²

   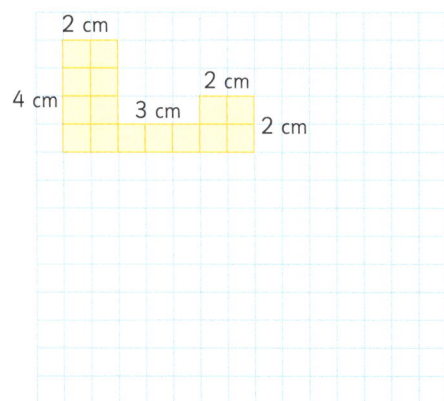

10. Draw the enlarged image of this shape, where all lengths are doubled.

Wednesday

1. Find the length of a cube with a volume of 216 cm^3. _____ cm

2. A square garden has a perimeter of 20 m. If you increase each length by a scale factor of 2, what is the new area of the garden? _____ m^2

3. Draw the enlarged image of this triangle, where all lengths are doubled.

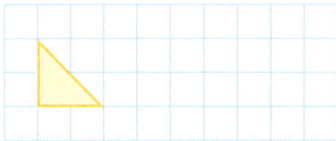

4. What would the volume of this cuboid be if you decreased all dimensions by 2.5 cm?

_____ cm^3

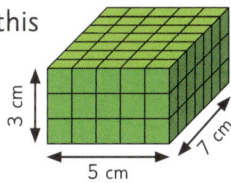
3 cm, 5 cm, 7 cm

5. Scale this rectangle by a factor of 2.

4 cm, 1 cm

6. A rectangle has a width of 9 cm and a length of 12 cm. What would the perimeter be if you enlarged the sides by a scale factor of 3? _____ cm

7. The volume of a cube is 64 cm^3. What would the volume be if all dimensions were enlarged by a scale factor of 2? _____ cm^3

8. Increasing the scale factor of a shape means enlarging the shape.

True ☐   False ☐

9. Double the dimensions of the cuboid and find the surface area of the new cuboid.

Area: _____ cm^2

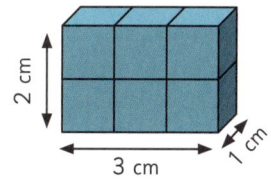
2 cm, 3 cm, 1 cm

10. Find the area of this irregular shape after its sides are increased by scale factor of 3.

_____ cm^2

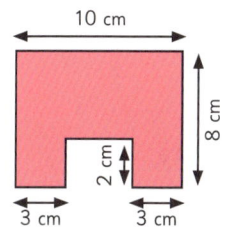
10 cm, 8 cm, 2 cm, 3 cm, 3 cm

Thursday

1. Doubling all the lengths of a rectangle is the same as increasing them by a scale factor of 2.

True ☐   False ☐

2. If each cube in this shape is 1 cm^3, what is the total volume? _____ cm^3

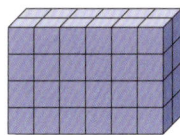

3. The volume of a cube is 216 cm^3 after its lengths were increased by a scale factor of 3. What was the volume of the original cube? _____ cm^3

4. A cuboid with a height of 4 cm, a length of 6cm and a width of 2 cm has all of its dimensions doubled. What is the surface area of the new shape? _____ cm^2

5. The sides of a square are 5 cm. When enlarged, each side measures 15 cm. What is the scale factor? _____

6. Complete the table for an enlarged cuboid.

	Length	Width	Height	Surface Area	Volume
Original	3 cm	2 cm	4 cm		24 cm^3
Enlargement	9 cm				

7. A square has an area of 16 cm^2. If each of its dimensions are scaled down by 0.5 cm, what is the new area of the square? _____ cm^2

8. Find the area of this shape if its lengths are increased by a scale factor of 2.

_____ cm^2

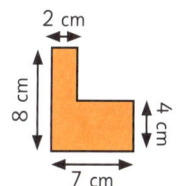
2 cm, 8 cm, 4 cm, 7 cm

9. A square garden bed has an area of 25 m^2. If you increase each side by a scale factor of 3, what is the new area of the garden? _____ m^2

10. Find the perimeter of the new garden. _____ m

1. $6a + 10 = 28$

   $a =$ _____

2. Increase €150 by 15%. €_____

3. A video game is on sale for €45. It originally cost €60. What is the percentage discount on the video game? _____

4. How many vertices has a hexagonal prism?

   _____

5. $3 + 0.145 + 2.17 =$ _____

6. Find the volume of the cuboid.

   _____ cm³

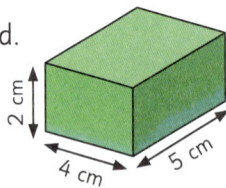

7. Find the surface area of the cuboid in question 6.

   _____ cm²

8. $532 \times 42 =$ _____

9. What coordinates would you have if you rotated (−3, −2) 180° about the point (0, 0)?

   _____

10. Enlarge this irregular shape by a scale factor of 2 and then find the area of the enlarged shape.

   Area: _____ cm²

Tuesday

1. Find the next three terms of the sequence.

   −12, −6, 0, _____, _____, _____

2. Find the missing term.

   0.4, 0.8, 1.6, _____, 6.4, 12.8

3. Maisie is three times the age of her younger brother, Leo, at the moment. If Leo is 3 years old, how old is Maisie?

   _____

4. What age will Maisie be when Leo is 10?

   _____

5. Write an expression to describe the relationship between Maisie's and Leo's ages.

   _____

6. Find the next three terms of this sequence.

   $\frac{1}{2}, \frac{1}{4}, \frac{1}{8}, \frac{1}{14},$ _____, _____, _____

7. Write an expression to show that a pizza is twice the price of a portion of chips.

   _____

8. Nathan is twice the height of his younger sister Mia. If Nathan is 1.54 m tall, how tall is Mia? _____ m

9. Write a rule to describe Nathan's height to Mia's height, at this moment in time.

   _____

10. Find then next two terms in this sequence.

   2%, 4%, 8%, 16%, _____, _____

Wednesday

1. Write an expression to show that a recipe needs three times as much sugar as it does butter.

   _____

2. Find the next three terms in this sequence.

   0.15, 0.30, 0.9, _____, _____, _____

3. 3 + 4 × 2 = 14

   True ☐   False ☐

4. A kitchen is 9 times the size of the utility room and the utility room is 6 m². Write an equation to show the relationship between the kitchen and the utility room.

   _____

5. Find the first 3 terms of this sequence.

   _____, _____, _____, $\frac{1}{12}$, $\frac{1}{15}$, $\frac{1}{18}$

6. Continue the sequence.

   A, C, E, G, _____, _____

7. Find the missing terms in this sequence.

   1.5, 1, _____, 0, –0.5, _____, –1.5

8. A school is selling tickets to a school play. Each ticket costs twice the price of parking. Write an expression to represent the total cost of the ticket and parking.

   _____

9. You eat three chocolates from a full box. Write an expression to describe this.

   _____

10. Sarah is saving money. She starts with €20 and saves an additional €5 each week. Write an equation that will show how much Sarah will have after 10 weeks. _____

Thursday

1. Find the missing terms in the sequence.

   1.5%, 3%, 4.5%, _____, _____, 9%

2. A dog weighs 12 kg and a cat weighs $\frac{1}{3}$ as much. What is the combined weight of the dog and the cat?

   _____ kg

3. Find the first three terms of this sequence.

   _____, _____, _____, 16, 25, 36

4. A gardener wants to create two square flower beds. One flower bed has an area of 3 m². The second bed is three times the size of the first. What is the area of the second bed? _____ m²

5. Continue the pattern.

   1, 3, 6, 10, _____, _____, _____

6. The first term in this sequence is –10.

   _____, –5, 0, 5, 10

   True ☐   False ☐

7. The starting term of a sequence is 3 and the difference between the consecutive terms is 0.4. What is the 4th term of the sequence?

   _____

8. A gold trophy is worth €20,000. This is twice the amount of a silver medal. Write a rule to describe this.

   _____

9. Continue the pattern.

   $\frac{1}{3}$, $\frac{1}{6}$, $\frac{1}{12}$, $\frac{1}{24}$, _____, _____

10. The first term in a sequence is 1 and there is 0.5 between each term. What is the 5th term of the sequence? _____

Friday | Week 1

1. Write 3,425,127 in expanded form using figures.

   _____

   _____

2. Use the Front-End strategy to ring the largest number and ✗ the smallest number.

   1,276,413   3,425,127   2,474,324

3. Round 3,425,127 to the nearest 10,000.

   _____

4. Write the values of the underlined digits in the number 1,835,638.15.

   _____

   _____

5. Round 12.635 to one decimal place. _____

6. Two hundred and fifty-one thousand, three hundred and forty-three is the same as 251,343.

   True ☐   False ☐

7. Model 126,353.21 on the notation board.

m	hth	tth	th	h	t	u	.	th	hth

8. What number is shown on the abacus?

   _____

   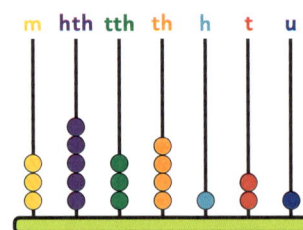

9. Write the number that is 4,000 greater than 34,275. _____

10. **Problem-Solving**

Croke Park had an attendance of 79,393 for a football semi-final. Round this number to the nearest hundred. _____

Friday | Week 2

1. 155 + 155 = _____

2. 44,777 + 220,810 + 5,676 = _____

3. Find the Front-End estimate for the following numbers.

   324   658,175   463   250,227

   _____   _____   _____   _____

4. Use the Place Value Partitioning strategy to solve 321,458 + 134,131. _____

5. 75,000 + 25,500 + 175,550 = _____

6. (12,264 + 25,765) − (10,345 + 15,136) =

   _____

7. Use the table to show the Clustering strategy when adding the numbers below.

Sum	Cluster	Rounding
240 + 400 + 175 + 350		
Estimate	**Actual**	**Difference**

8. Use the Constant Different strategy to find the difference between 400,000 and 354,281.

   _____

9. The area of Italy is 301,340 km². The area of France is 551,695 km². Find the difference between the two areas. _____ km²

10. **Problem-Solving**

Emily won €40,000 in the Lotto jackpot. She decides to buy a car for €25,475 and pay off a loan of €10,236. How much money does she have left? €_____

1. Complete the table below.

Number	hth	tth	th	h	t	u	.	$\frac{1}{10}$	$\frac{1}{100}$	$\frac{1}{1,000}$
					1	8	.	4	6	5
×1,000							.			
×10,000							.			

2. 171.75 × 100 = _____

3. A teacher buys whiteboard markers for her class. She buys 256 packs, and each pack contains 18 markers. How many markers will she have in total?

_____

4. 219 × 64 = _____

5. A film production company needs to hire 245 crew members for a film project. If each crew member is paid €750, how much will the work cost in total?

€_____

6. 185 × 18 = _____

7. 1,235 × 24 = _____

8. 0.4 × 10 = 40

True ☐   False ☐

9. 173.25 × 100 = _____

10. Problem-Solving

A class of 24 students are going on a school tour. Each student pays €55 for the trip. How much money will be collected in total from all the students? €_____

1. Ring the triangular numbers and draw an ✗ through the square numbers.

3   10   15   16   21   36

2. $\sqrt{25} + \sqrt{36}$ = _____

3. 2^4 = _____

4. Complete the table below.

2^2	2 × 2	4
3^2		
4^3		
5^3		

5. The 2nd, 4th and 6th terms in a sequence are 200, 600 and 1,000. What are the 1st, 3rd and 5th terms in the sequence?

_____, _____, _____

6. 2.0, 1.85, 1.70, 1.55, _____, _____, _____

7. $2^3 + \sqrt{100}$ = _____

8. Plot points to represent the first four triangular numbers on the graph below.

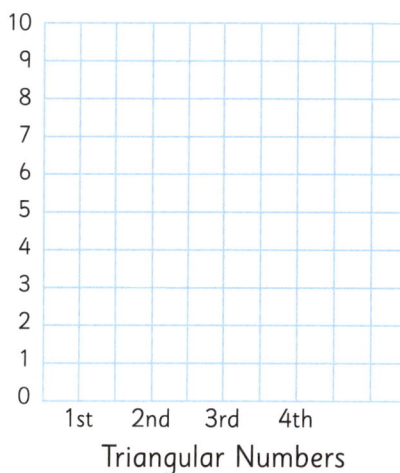

Triangular Numbers

9. Complete the following pattern

A1, B2, C3, D4, _____, _____, _____

10. Problem-Solving

Hugo is making fruit baskets. He adds fruit in the following pattern: The first basket has 2 apples, the second has 4 apples, the third basket has 6 apples and the fourth basket has 8 apples. How many apples will be in the tenth basket? _____

Friday | Week 5

1. Complete the table.

	th	h	t	u	.	$\frac{1}{10}$	$\frac{1}{100}$	$\frac{1}{1,000}$	$\frac{1}{10,000}$
		7	5	2	.	3			
÷ 10					.				
÷ 100					.				
÷ 1,000					.				
÷ 10,000					.				

2. 923 ÷ 71 = _____

3. 171.75 ÷ 100 = _____

4. A prize pot of €16,380 was shared equally between 18 winners. How much did each winner receive? €_____

5. 57.6 ÷ 4 = _____

6. 526 ÷ 32 = _____

7. 42,000 ÷ 6,000 = _____

8. 12.186 ÷ 100 = 0.12186

True ☐   False ☐

9. 943 ÷ 41 = _____

10. **Problem-Solving**

A rainwater tank holds 960 litres of water. How many times can 15 litres of water be drawn from it? _____

Friday | Week 6

1. −10 > −8

True ☐   False ☐

2. Complete the table of golf scores. Par is 72. Par is the target number of strokes it should take to get the ball around the golf course. The person with the lowest score is the winner.

Oliver took 68 strokes in Round 1. 68 is 4 less than 72 (par) so his score is −4. He took 72 strokes in Round 2, so he gets par, which adds 0 to his score. In Round 3, he took 73 strokes, which is one more than par, so his score is 1.

Name	Round 1	Round 2	Round 3	Total Score
Oliver	−4	0 (par)	+1	−3
Ivy	−2	+3	−3	
Jack	0 (par)	−1	+2	

3. Who won the golfing competition?

_____

4. Who lost the golfing competition?

_____

5. How many strokes did Ivy take in Round 1?

_____

6. How many strokes did Jack take over all 3 rounds?

_____

7. What was the difference between Jack's and Oliver's total scores?

_____

8. −8 − 7 = _____

9. −3 + 2 − 6 = _____

10. **Problem-Solving**

Maria is tracking the daily temperature. On Monday, the temperature was 5°C. On Tuesday, the temperature dropped by 8°C. On Wednesday, the temperature rose by 3°C from Tuesday's temperature. What was the temperature on Wednesday? _____

1. Colour in $\frac{3}{5}$ of the shape.

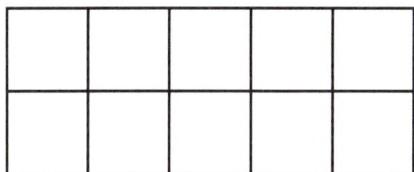

2. Find $\frac{4}{5}$ of 80. _____

3. Simplify $\frac{16}{20}$. _____

4. Write $2\frac{3}{6}$ as an improper fraction. _____

5. Write $\frac{32}{7}$ as a mixed number. _____

6. Tick the correct answer. $\frac{3}{5} + \frac{1}{3} =$

   $\frac{4}{8}$ ☐

   $\frac{3}{25}$ ☐

   $\frac{14}{15}$ ☐

7. $3\frac{2}{5} + 1\frac{4}{8} =$ _____

8. $5\frac{1}{4} - 3\frac{2}{3} =$ _____

9. (a) $\frac{4}{5} - \frac{2}{3} =$ _____

   (b) $\frac{2}{3} - \frac{3}{5} =$ _____

10. **Problem-Solving**

    A pizza is divided into 12 slices. Jamie eats $\frac{2}{3}$ of it and Alex eats $\frac{1}{6}$. How many slices are left? _____

    Represent this using a model of your choice.

1. $10 \div \frac{4}{5} =$ _____

2. $\frac{3}{8} \times \frac{2}{4} =$ _____

3. Pippa spends $\frac{2}{3}$ of her money on clothes. She has €24 left. How much did she start with?

   €_____

4. (a) How many quarters are in 20? _____

   (b) How many thirds are in 18? _____

5. Simplify $\frac{15}{20}$. _____

6. Write the ratio of sweets to lollipops in its simplest form.

   _____

7. $5\frac{2}{7} + 1\frac{1}{2} =$ _____

8. $5\frac{1}{2} - 3\frac{2}{4} =$ _____

9. Write $5\frac{3}{8}$ as an improper fraction. _____

10. **Problem-Solving**

    A cake recipe uses 100 g of flour for every 140 g of sugar. Write this as a ratio in its simplest form. _____

1. Fill in the table.

mm	cm	m
	75 cm	
		1.32 m
264 mm		

2. This pencil is _____ cm long.

3. Find the perimeter of this square.

_____ cm

3.5 cm
3.5 cm

4. Moana cuts a 25 cm long piece of string into 5 equal pieces. How many mm long is each piece? _____ mm

5. 435 mm + 17 cm + 0.64 m = _____ m

6. Draw a line measuring 73 mm.

7. Draw a rectangle with a width of 1.5 cm and a length of 6 cm.

8. Write the correct symbol (>, < or =).

2.08 km ☐ 800 m

9. What is the perimeter of the flowerbed?

_____ m

1.5 m
3 m

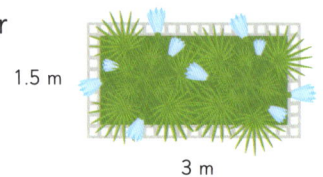

10. **Problem-Solving**

David ran $\frac{5}{8}$ of the race. If he ran 3,000 m, how long is the race in total? _____ km

1. Complete the table.

Length	Width	Perimeter	Area
8 cm	7 cm		
14 cm	6 cm		
23.5 cm	5 cm		

2. Find the surface area of this triangular prism.

_____ cm^2

5 cm
4 cm
8 cm
6 cm

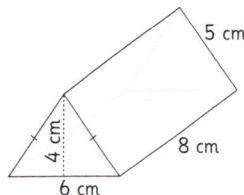

3. Find the area of this irregular shape.

_____ cm^2

3 cm
5 cm
6 cm
2.5 cm

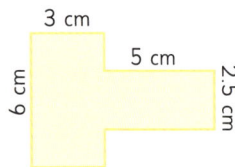

4. The area of a triangle is half its base times its height.

True ☐   False ☐

5. Draw a shape with a perimeter of 20 cm and an area of 16 cm^2.

6. A rectangular flowerbed measures 8 metres in length and 5 metres in width. Find the total area of the flower bed. _____ m^2

7. Find the surface area of a cuboid with dimensions 6 cm, 3 cm and 2 cm. _____ cm^2.

8. 57,100 m^2 = _____ hectares

9. Using a scale of 1 cm to 3 m, draw a playground measuring 6 m by 4 m.

10. **Problem-Solving**

$\frac{2}{5}$ of a 80 m^2 garden is covered by grass. How many square metres are not covered? _____ m^2

Friday — Week 11

1. Complete the table.

Standard Decimal Form	Expanded Decimal Form	Decimal Fraction Form	Expanded Decimal Fraction Form
1.275			
		$\frac{3751}{1000}$	
	2 + 0.7 + 0.03 + 0.008		
			$4 + \frac{5}{10} + \frac{8}{100} + \frac{3}{1000}$

2. Round 3.8613 to the nearest tenth, hundredth and thousandth.

$\frac{1}{10}$ _____ $\frac{1}{100}$ _____ $\frac{1}{1000}$ _____

3. $18 - 6.53 + 7.642 =$ _____

4. $\frac{2}{5}$ m + 0.35 m − 0.16 m = _____ m

5. A carpenter cuts a plank into three lengths: 1.3 m, $1\frac{29}{100}$ m and 1.73 m. Find the average length of the three planks. _____ m

6. Ella spends 0.25 of her money in one shop and $\frac{2}{10}$ of her money in another shop. If she has €33 left, how much did she start with? €_____

7. Round 6.753 to one decimal place. _____

8. Write the correct symbol (>, < or =).

2.3 ☐ $2\frac{3}{10}$

9. $6\frac{2}{4} + 5.95 - 1\frac{1}{5} =$ _____

10. Problem-Solving

Masha spends €28.50 a month on credit for her phone. Sylvia spends twice this amount. How much does Sylvia spend? €_____

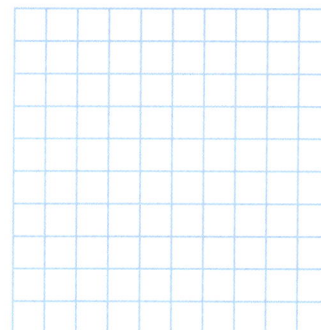

Friday — Week 12

1. Fill in the table.

Simplified Fraction	Decimal Fraction	Decimal	Percentage
$\frac{3}{4}$			
			35%
	$\frac{25}{100}$		
		0.15	

2. Find 24% of 80. _____

3. 18% = 1.8   True ☐   False ☐

4. 15% of 180 = _____

5. Write the correct symbol (>, < or =).

$66\frac{2}{3}$% ☐ $\frac{2}{3}$

6. Use three different colours to shade in 22%, $\frac{1}{4}$ and 0.37 of the grid. What percentage of the grid remains unshaded? _____

7. Decrease 90 by $33\frac{1}{3}$%. _____

8. 25% of 60 is 15.

True ☐   False ☐

9. Ring the amount that is 25% of 360.

90   85   80

10. Problem-Solving

In a school, 30 out of 150 pupils wear glasses. What percentage of pupils wear glasses? _____

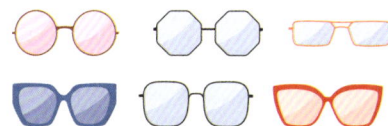

1. The table below represents how Sixth Class pupils travel to school. Use the information to draw a tally chart.

	Number	Tally
Cycle	6	
Walk	6	
Bus	8	
Car	10	

2. Draw a bar chart to represent the data above.

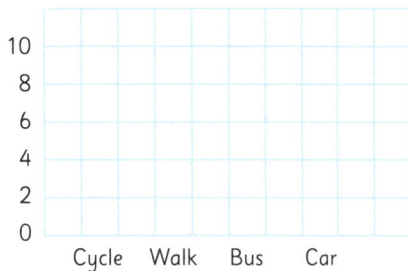

3. Which modes of transport are the same in number? _____

4. How many pupils are in Sixth Class altogether? _____

5. What percentage of pupils cycle to school? _____

6. What is the most popular mode of transport for getting to school? _____

7. Find the range for the modes of transport. _____

8. What fraction of pupils walk or cycle to school? _____

9. Find the median number for the modes of transport. _____

10. **Problem-Solving**
Find the ratio of pupils who take the bus to the pupils who cycle. _____

1. The marks received by 6 students in a test are: 75, 80, 83, 70, 90, 88. What is the range in the test results? _____

2. What was the average test result? _____

3. Draw a pie chart to represent the favourite fruits in a class of 20 pupils.

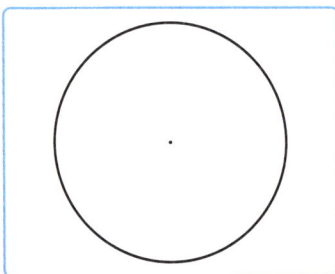

Apples: 30%

Bananas: 25%

Oranges: 20%

Grapes: 15%

Other fruits: 10%

4. How many pupils in the class preferred grapes? _____

5. How many more pupils preferred apples to bananas? _____

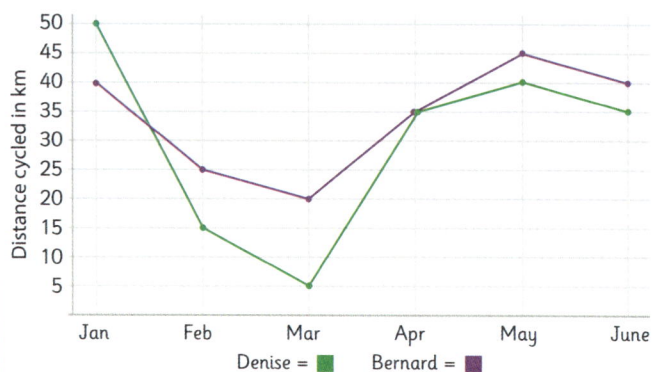

6. How far did both Denise and Bernard cycle in total? _____ km

7. What distance did Denise average over the 6 months? _____ km

8. Which month did both Bernard and Denise cycle the same distance? _____

9. On which months did Bernard cycle the same distances? _____

10. **Problem-Solving**
The ages of five friends are 12, 15, 13, 16, and 14 years. What is the range of their ages? _____

Friday | Week 15

1. The diameter of a circle is 15 cm. What is its radius? _____ cm

2. Find $\frac{5}{6}$ of 360°. _____ °

3. Label the parts of the circle.

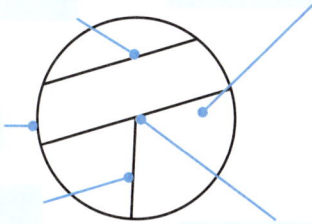

4. Find the value of the missing angle in this irregular pentagon.

   _____ °

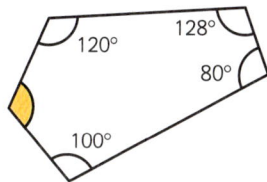

5. All angles in a quadrilateral add up to 360°.

   True ☐   False ☐

6. The radius of a circle is 4 cm. Find its circumference. _____ cm

7. The angles in an irregular pentagon do not add up to 540°.

   True ☐   False ☐

8. Find the value of the missing angle.

   _____ °

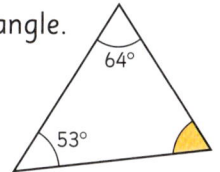

9. Ring the correct answer. A pentagon is made up of:

   2 triangles   3 triangles   2 squares

10. **Problem-Solving**

A large square has a side of 10 cm. Inside it, there is a smaller square with a side of 4 cm. What is the area of the remaining part of the large square after removing the small square? _____ cm²

Friday | Week 16

1. Ireland is 5 hours ahead of New York time. If it is 6:23 p.m. in Ireland, what time is it in New York?

   _____

2. 2 hrs 10 mins × 5 = ____ hr _____ mins

3. How many minutes are in 5 hours 33 mins?

   _____

4. Write 18:17 in the 12-hour format.

   _____

5. 7 hrs 10 mins − 6 hrs 45 mins =
   ____ hr _____ mins

6. There are 180 minutes in 3 hours.

   True ☐   False ☐

7. A flight leaves Cork at 1:15 p.m. and arrives in London at 2:40 p.m. How long is the flight?

   ____ hr _____ mins

8. How many degrees are between the two hands on the clock?

   _____ °

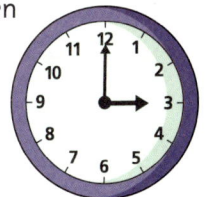

9. 2 hrs 45 mins + 3 hrs 35 mins =

   ____ hr _____ mins

10. **Problem-Solving**

Jade reads her book for 45 minutes every morning and for 25 minutes every night. How many hours and minutes does she spend reading her book each day? ____ hr _____ mins

1. Complete the table.

Time	Speed	Distance
3 hours		210 km
	18 km/h	63 km
2 hours	122.5 km/h	

2. A film starts at 18:25 and finishes at 21:05. How long is the film?

____ hr ____ mins

3. 19:25 is the same time as 7:25 a.m.

True ☐   False ☐

4. Rena runs 4 km in 30 minutes. How long will it take her to run 10 km? ____ hr ____ mins

5. A train travels at an average speed of 160 km/h. How long will it take to travel 400 km? ____ hr ____ mins

6. What is your average speed if you cycle 54 km in 3 hours? _____ km/h

7. What is your average speed if you drive 160 km in 2.5 hours? _____ km/h

8. Convert 1:17 p.m. to 24-hour format. _____

9. How many minutes are in 2 hours 43 minutes? Ring the correct answer.

103 mins   163 mins   153 mins

10. Problem-Solving

It takes Mark 48 minutes to walk 5 km. It will take Niamh $\frac{1}{3}$ longer to walk the same distance. How long does it take Niamh? ____ hr ____ mins

1. Model 3 × 0.2 on the grid below.

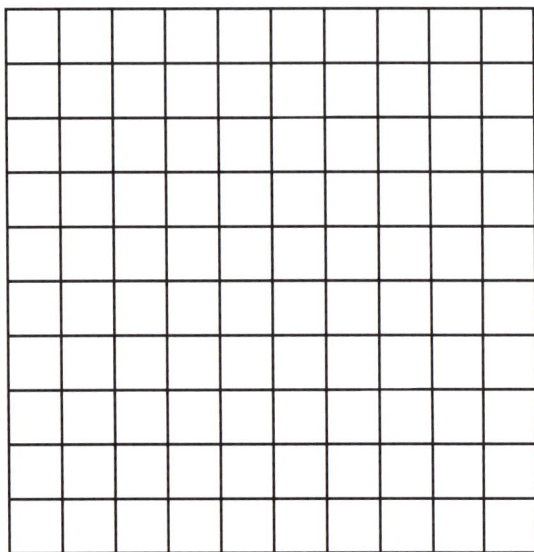

2. What number is 7.34 times greater than 3.7?

_____

3. 0.8 × 0.8 = 6.4

True ☐   False ☐

4. Deirdre earns €85.75 each day. How much will she earn in 28 days? €_____

5. 24.7 × 6.8 = _____

6. 133.57 × 1,000 = _____

7. A packet of colouring pencils costs €3.50. Mia has €10. How many packets can she buy? _____

8. 28.18 × 4.5 = _____

9. Find the area of a basketball court that has a length of 27.9 m and a width of 14.8 m. _____ m²

10. Problem-Solving

The Sixth Class school tour costs €57.60 per pupil. If 26 pupils are going, what is the total cost of the tour? €_____

Friday | Week 19

1. $\frac{2}{3}m = 6$

   $m = $ _____

2. $(54 \div 6) \times 12 = $ _____

3. $3a + 4 = 25$

   $a = $ _____

4. $4^2 + 6^2 = $ _____

5. $7x = 21$

   $x = $ _____

6. $7 \times (84 \div 12) = $ _____

7. $5 \times 5 + 6 = 55$

   True ☐   False ☐

8. $45.15 \div 5 \times 3 = $ _____

9. $9 \times 7 - 10 = $ _____

10. **Problem-Solving**
    Write an expression to show an order for 2 pizzas and 3 colas.

    _____

Friday | Week 20

1. Which is it better value?

   one box of chocolates for €3.70 ☐

   three boxes of chocolates for €10.50 ☐

2. A plumber charges €27 an hour before VAT. How much will she charge for 2 hours of work after 13.5% VAT is added?

   €_____

3. Different countries can charge different VAT rates.

   True ☐   False ☐

4. Sarah buys a games console for €249. This included 23% VAT. Rounding to the nearest cent, how much did the console cost before VAT was added?

   €_____

5. Find 23% of €352. €_____

6. Which is better value?

   500 g of sweets for €1.50 ☐

   2 kg of sweets for €5.00 ☐

7. Mia buys a car for €8,400. This included 23% VAT. Rounding to the nearest cent, how much did the car cost before VAT was added?

   €_____

8. VAT of 23% is added to a copy book costing €2.00. How much does the copy book cost after VAT is added?

   €_____

9. Which is better value?

   10 l of paint for €52.50 ☐

   5 l of paint for €25.50 ☐

10. **Problem-Solving**
    A group ticket to an amusement park costs €120.
    This includes 13.5% VAT. Rounding to the nearest cent, how much VAT was charged on the ticket? €_____

1. A farmer buys 10 bags of grain for €200. If she sells each bag for €25, how much profit will she make?
   €_____

2. If a video game costs 60 USD in the United States, and the exchange rate is 1 USD = 1.2 AUD, how much will the video game cost in AUD? _____

3. If 1 AUD equals 0.70 USD and Lisa has 35 AUD, approximately how many USD does she have? _____

4. If 500 JPY equals 4.50 USD, what is the exchange rate from JYP to USD? _____

5. Find the total amount of interest earned on an €11,000 investment with a simple interest of 3.5% over 3 years. €_____

6. If a bakery sells cakes worth €2,000 and the total cost of ingredients and labour is €1,500, what is the percentage profit? _____

7. You invest €500 at a compound interest rate of 4% per year for 2 years. What will the total amount be at the end of the investment period? €_____

8. A wholesaler sells 50 kg of apples for €1,000. If the wholesaler's cost was €800, what profit and percentage profit did they make?

   _____   _____

9. 'Compound Interest' and 'Simple Interest' mean the same thing.

   True ☐   False ☐

10. **Problem-Solving**
    One box of 10 pencils costs €5.00 and one box of 15 pencils costs €6.00. Which is better value for money? _____

1. Model $0.6 \div 0.3$ on the grid below.

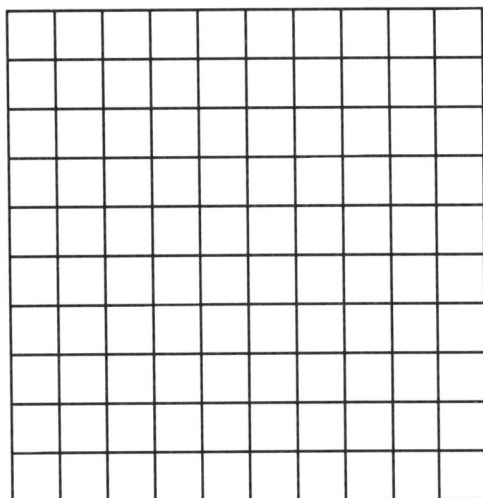

2. How many times is 0.48 contained in 4.32?
   _____

3. $4.9 \div 0.07 = 7$

   True ☐   False ☐

4. $7.506 \div 2.78 =$ _____

5. Aoife is cutting sheets of wrapping paper measuring 0.75 m from a roll measuring 6 m. How many sheets will she be able to cut? _____

6. $1.735 \div 0.01 =$ _____

7. $12 \div 0.8 =$ _____

8. How many times can 2.3 be taken from 3.496? _____

9. $9.731 \div 0.37 =$ _____

10. **Problem-Solving**
    Diesel costs €1.78 per litre. Samir pays €62.30 to fill his tank. How many litres did he buy?
    _____ l

1. Draw an angle measuring 215°.

2. Use your protractor to measure this angle.

_____ °

3. How many degrees is the angle shown on the clock?

_____ °

4. When turning clockwise, there are 45° between the north and north-east points on a compass.

True ☐   False ☐

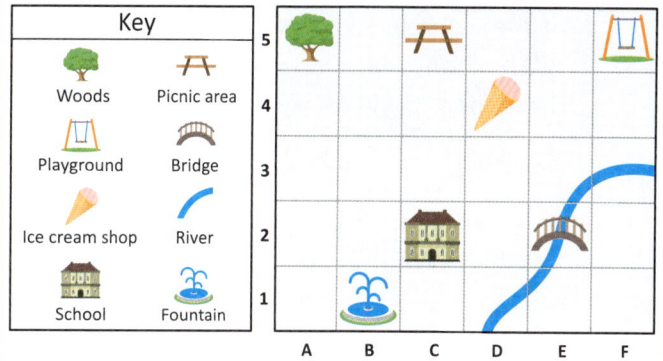

Key

Woods   Picnic area
Playground   Bridge
Ice cream shop   River
School   Fountain

5. Find the coordinates of the fountain. _____

6. Find the coordinates of the playground. _____

7. Which direction would you walk to go from the school to the picnic area? _____

8. Where is the picnic area in relation to the woods? _____

9. Find the coordinates of the ice cream shop.

_____

10. **Problem-Solving**

If you are in F2 and cross the bridge, what are your new coordinates? _____

1. In a pair of coordinates, the x-coordinate always comes first.

True ☐   False ☐

2. A floor plan shows a school hall with a length of 12 cm and a width of 4 cm. If the scale is 1 cm = 2.5 m, what are the actual dimensions of the room in metres? _____

3. What is the area of the room in question 2?

_____ m²

4. Longitude lines run east to west.

True ☐   False ☐

5. Latitude lines measure how far north or south a place is from the equator.

True ☐   False ☐

6. Plot the coordinates (–5, 3) and (5, –3) on the grid below and draw a line to join the two points.

7. Draw a quadrilateral of your choice in the top right quadrant of the grid.

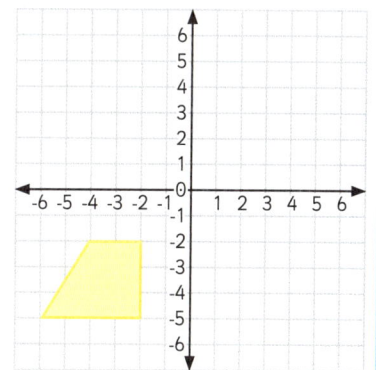

8. List the coordinates for the vertices of your quadrilateral.

_____, _____, _____, _____

9. List the coordinates for the vertices of the yellow shape.

_____, _____, _____, _____

10. **Problem-Solving**

A bedroom is 3 cm by 4 cm on a floor plan. The scale is 1 cm = 2 m, what is the area? _____ m²

1. If the weather forecast says there is a 70% chance of rain tomorrow, what is the likelihood it will rain?

   Unlikely ☐   Likely ☐   Certain ☐

2. A jar contains 5 yellow, 6 green and 9 purple marbles. What is the probability of randomly selecting a green marble? _____

3. A farmer has a basket with 10 apples and 5 oranges. If he picks one fruit at random, what is the probability that it is not an apple? _____

4. If you flip a coin, what is the probability of getting tails?

   $\frac{1}{4}$ ☐ $\frac{1}{2}$ ☐ $\frac{1}{3}$ ☐ $\frac{3}{4}$ ☐

5. There are 10 prizes and 50 tickets in a lucky draw contest. What is the probability of winning a prize if you buy one ticket? _____

6. If you roll two dice, what is the probability that the sum of the numbers is 8? _____

7. There are 18 girls in a class of 30 students. If a student is chosen at random, what is the probability that the student is a boy? _____

8. What is the probability of rolling an even number with a standard dice throw? _____

9. A jar contains 5 red lollipops, 3 blue lollipops and 2 green lollipops. If you pick a lollipop at random, what is the probability it is blue?

   _____

10. **Problem-Solving**

    You have 6 black socks and 4 white socks in a drawer. If you pick two socks at random, what is the probability that both are black? _____

1. Daniel has 5 books weighing 1.2 kg, 1.5 kg, 1.8 kg, 2.0 kg and 1.0 kg. If he leaves the heaviest book at home, what is the total weight of the books he takes to school? _____ kg

2. Express 300 g as a fraction of 1.2 kg. _____

3. 1 kg of feathers is lighter than 1 kg of coal.

   True ☐   False ☐

4. If a rabbit weighs 2 kg and a tortoise weighs 8 kg, what is the simplest ratio of the rabbit's weight to the tortoise's weight? _____

5. Convert 2,500 grams into kilograms.

   2.5 kg ☐   25 kg ☐

   0.25 kg ☐   250 kg ☐

6. You're ordering pizzas for a party. Each pizza weighs about 1.5 kg. If you want to serve 10 pizzas, what is the total weight of the pizzas?

   _____ kg

7. A chef prepares a meal by combining 0.5 kg of pasta, 1.2 kg of sauce and 0.3 kg of cheese. What is the total weight the meal?

   _____ kg

8. A basketball weighs 620 g. How much does the basketball weigh in kg? _____ kg

9. You prepare a 1.5 kg casserole for a dinner party. If each guest can eat a 250 g serving, how many guests can you serve? _____

10. **Problem-Solving**

    A feather weighs approximately 0.008 kg and a standard brick weighs 1.8 kg. How many feathers would you need to equal the weight of the brick? _____

1. Find the volume of a cuboid with length 12 cm, height 8 cm and width 4 cm. _____ cm³

2. The volume of a cube is 216 cm³. If the height is 6 cm and the length is 6 cm, what is the width? _____ cm

3. The volume of a cuboid is 80 cm³. If the length is 5 cm and the height is 8 cm, what is the width? _____ cm

4. Convert 0.3 litres to ml. _____ ml

5. Find $\frac{2}{5}$ of 4 l. _____ l

6. Find 35% of 300 ml. _____ ml

7. Calculate 65% of 1,000 ml. _____ ml

8. 2 ml + 0.25 l × 3 l = ____ ml

9. Oliver used 0.45 of a tin of red paint, Daniel used $\frac{1}{3}$ of a tin of blue paint and Jack used 70% of a tin of pink paint. Work out how much paint each boy used as a fraction, a decimal and percentage.

	ml	Fractional Form	Decimal Form	Percentage
Red Paint (200 ml)			0.45	
Blue Paint (220 ml)		$\frac{1}{3}$		
Pink Paint (330 ml)				70%

10. **Problem-Solving**

   Dean's bottle holds 0.375 l of water. How many 15 ml teaspoons would it take to fill the bottle? _____

1. Complete the table.

	Name	No. of Faces	Type of Faces	No. of Edges	No. of Vertices

2. A square-based pyramid has 5 faces.

   True ☐   False ☐

3. Which 3-D shape does this net make? _____

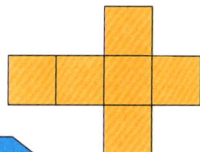

4. Name this 3-D shape.

   _____

5. Draw the net of a triangular-based prism.

6. Draw the right-side view of this shape.

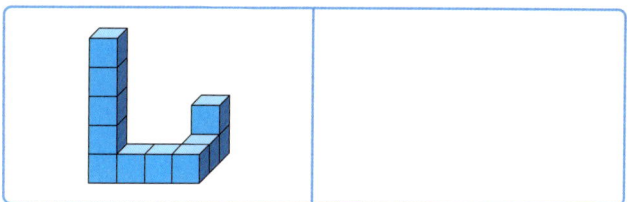

7. I have 2 pentagonal faces and 5 rectangular faces. What shape am I? _____

8. How many vertices does a cube have? _____

9. A cuboid has 8 vertices. True ☐   False ☐

10. **Problem-Solving**

   A cube and a triangular prism are stacked. How many faces does this new 3-D shape have? _____

Friday Week 29

1. Find the value of y if $3y \times 4 = 24$. _____

2. Colour all the prime numbers.

1	2	3	4	5	6
7	8	9	10	11	12
13	14	15	16	17	18
19	20	21	22	23	24
25	26	27	28	29	30
31	32	33	34	35	36

3. (a) List one set of twin prime numbers.

   _____

   (b) List one set of cousin prime numbers.

   _____

4. Write the next 2 terms in this sequence.

   4   9   16   25   _____   _____

5. Find the HCF of 15 and 40. _____

6. Find the LCM of 15 and 40. _____

7. (a) $\frac{1}{4}r = 4$. Find the value of r. _____

   (b) $\frac{2}{3}b = 8$. Find the value of b. _____

   (c) $\frac{3}{5}a = 9$. Find the value of a. _____

8. $x = 3$, $y = 4$. Find the value of $3x + 4y$. _____

9. Find the value of x if $2x + 3 = 15$. _____

10. **Problem-Solving**

    Write a word problem for $3w + 2 = 28$. _____

Friday Week 30

1. Draw the other half of this shape.

2. A scalene triangle has a rotational symmetry of 3.

   True ☐   False ☐

3. Name a shape with a rotational symmetry of order 4. _____

4. Draw the mirror image of this pattern.

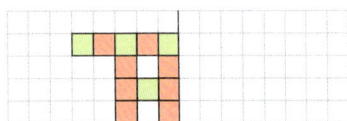

5. Write the coordinates of this triangle if it was rotated 180° about the point (0,0).

   A′ _____

   B′ _____

   C′ _____

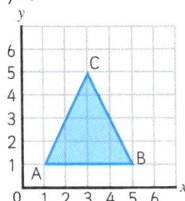

6. Draw the lines of symmetry in these shapes.

7. Rotate the triangle 180° about the point (0,0).

   A′ _____

   B′ _____

   C′ _____

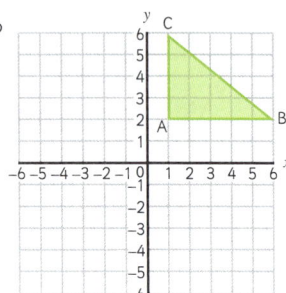

8. Ring the shape that has no order of rotational symmetry.

9. Draw the other half of this shape.

10. **Problem-Solving**

    One square in a tessellation has a side length of 4 cm.

    (a) Work out the area of one square. _____ cm^2

    (b) Work out the area of a tessellated pattern made from 6 squares. _____ cm^2

1. Enlarge this shape by a scale factor of 2.

2. What would the dimensions of this triangle be if it was increased by a scale factor of 2?

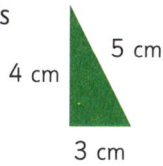

4 cm · 5 cm · 3 cm

_____

3. Find the area of the enlarged triangle from question 2. _____ cm^2

4. Complete the table using the original triangle from question 2.

Scale Factor	Perimeter
1	
2	
3	

5. Graph the perimeters of each triangle using the table from question 4.

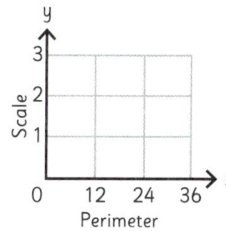

y · 3 · 2 · 1 · Scale · 0 · 12 · 24 · 36 · x · Perimeter

6. If each cube in this cuboid is 1 cm^3, what is the total volume?

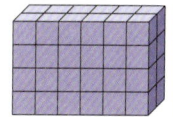

_____ cm^3

7. What is the surface area of the cuboid?

_____ cm

8. A rectangle has a width of 8 m and a length of 4 cm. What would the area be if you decreased its lengths by a scale factor of 2? _____ cm^2

9. The formula for the volume of a cube is length × width × height.

True ☐   False ☐

10. **Problem-Solving**

The volume of a cube is 64 cm^3. What would the volume be if all dimensions were decreased by a scale factor of 2? _____ cm^3

1. Identify the 7th term in this sequence.

2, 4, 8, 16, 32, _, _____

2. Write the next three terms in this sequence.

0.2, 0.4, 0.7, 1.1, _____, _____, _____

3. Write a rule to describe the sequence in question 2. _____

4. The next term in this sequence is 2.5.

0.25, 1, 1.75, _

True ☐   False ☐

5. Continue the sequence.

−28, −14, 0, _____, _____, _____

6. Find the missing term in this sequence.

$\frac{1}{8}$, $\frac{1}{16}$, _____, $\frac{1}{64}$

7. Find the next three terms in this sequence.

1 + 2 = 3,   2 + 3 = 5,   3 + 4 = 7

_____, _____, _____

8. What is the 10th term in the sequence?

0.1, 0.3, 0.5, 0.7, 0.9, _, _, _, _, _____

9. Draw the next term in the sequence.

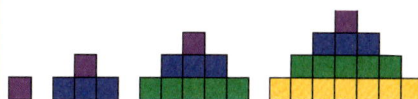

10. **Problem-Solving**

The starting point in a sequence is 5 and the difference between each consecutive term is 0.35. What is the 7th term in the sequence? _____

100 Square

1	2	3	4	5	6	7	8	9	10
11	12	13	14	15	16	17	18	19	20
21	22	23	24	25	26	27	28	29	30
31	32	33	34	35	36	37	38	39	40
41	42	43	44	45	46	47	48	49	50
51	52	53	54	55	56	57	58	59	60
61	62	63	64	65	66	67	68	69	70
71	72	73	74	75	76	77	78	79	80
81	82	83	84	85	86	87	88	89	90
91	92	93	94	95	96	97	98	99	100

Multiplication Chart

×	1	2	3	4	5	6	7	8	9	10	11	12
1	1	2	3	4	5	6	7	8	9	10	11	12
2	2	4	6	8	10	12	14	16	18	20	22	24
3	3	6	9	12	15	18	21	24	27	30	33	36
4	4	8	12	16	20	24	28	32	36	40	44	48
5	5	10	15	20	25	30	35	40	45	50	55	60
6	6	12	18	24	30	36	42	48	54	60	66	72
7	7	14	21	28	35	42	49	56	63	70	77	84
8	8	16	24	32	40	48	56	64	72	80	88	96
9	9	18	27	36	45	54	63	72	81	90	99	108
10	10	20	30	40	50	60	70	80	90	100	110	120
11	11	22	33	44	55	66	77	88	99	110	121	132
12	12	24	36	48	60	72	84	96	108	120	132	144

Fraction Wall

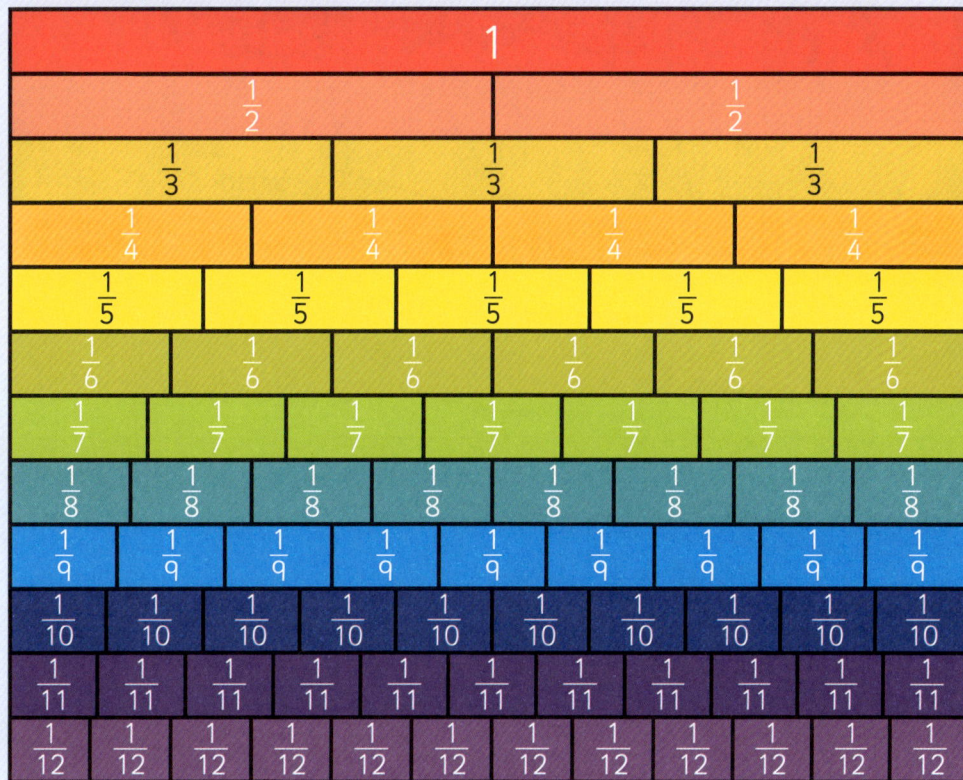

BIDMAS

Brackets ( )

Indices

Division ÷

Multiplication ×

Addition +

Subtraction −

We use BIDMAS to remember the order of mathematical operations.

Number Line

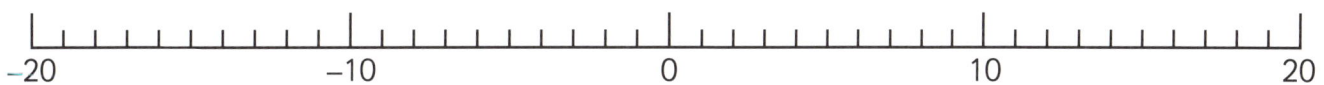

Parts of a Circle

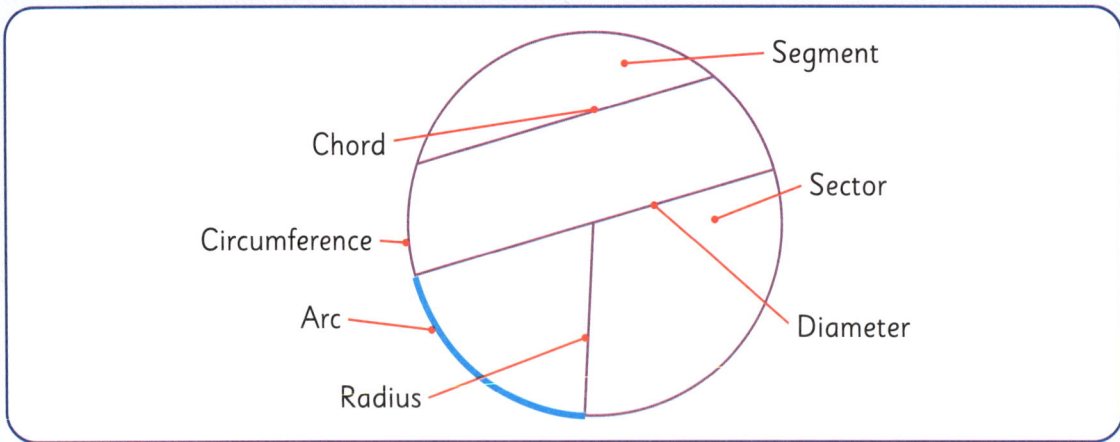

Segment

Chord

Sector

Circumference

Diameter

Arc

Radius

Conversion Chart

Weight	
1 kg	1,000 g
$\frac{3}{4}$ kg	750 g
$\frac{1}{2}$ kg	500 g
$\frac{1}{4}$ kg	250 g
Distance	
1 km	1,000 m
$\frac{3}{4}$ km	750 m
$\frac{1}{2}$ km	500 m
$\frac{1}{4}$ km	250 m
1 m	100 cm
$\frac{3}{4}$ m	75 cm
$\frac{1}{2}$ m	50 cm
$\frac{1}{4}$ m	25 cm
Volume	
1 l	1,000 ml
$\frac{3}{4}$ l	750 ml
$\frac{1}{2}$ l	500 ml
$\frac{1}{4}$ l	250 ml

Maths Dictionary

Number and Operations

Decimal: a number that uses a decimal point to show parts of a whole (e.g. 0.5).

Percentage: a number out of 100. For example, 25% means 25 out of 100.

Place Value: the value of a digit depending on where it is in a number (e.g. in 345, the 4 is worth 40).

Factor: a number that divides exactly into another number (e.g. 2 is a factor of 8).

Multiple: a number that is the result of multiplying a number by a whole number (e.g. 15 is a multiple of 5).

Remainder: the amount left over after dividing (e.g. $13 \div 4 = 3$ remainder 1).

Algebra and Equations

Variable: a letter or symbol that stands for a number in Maths. We often use the letter x as a variable, but variables can be any letter.

Indice: the exponent or power that indicates how many times a number is multiplied by itself.

Equation: a number sentence with an equals sign, showing that two things are the same (e.g. $4 + 3 = 7$).

Expression: a number sentence without an equals sign (e.g. $3 \times a + 2$).

Data and Chance

Data: information that we collect, count or measure.

Bar Chart: a graph that uses bars to show amounts.

Pictogram: a chart that uses pictures or symbols to show data.

Tally Sheet: a simple form used to record and count data or occurrences, typically using marks or tally lines to represent quantities.

Trend Graph: a visual representation that shows the direction and pattern of data points over a period of time, illustrating how variables change or evolve.

Comparison Chart: a visual representation that displays the differences or similarities between two or more items, categories or groups.

Probability: the chance of something happening.

Likely / Unlikely: words to describe how probable something is.

Certain / Impossible: certain means it will definitely happen. Impossible means it cannot happen.

Measures and Geometry

Perimeter: the total distance around the outside of a shape.

Surface Area: the total area covered by the outer surfaces of a 3-D object.

Volume: the amount of space occupied by a 3-D object.

Transformation: a change to a shape by moving, flipping or turning it.

Translation: moving a shape to a new place without turning it.

Reflection: flipping a shape to make a mirror image.

Rotation: turning a shape around a point.

Coordinate: a pair of numbers that shows where a point is on a grid (e.g. (3, 2)).

Angle: the space between two lines that meet at a point, measured in degrees.

Acute Angle: an angle smaller than a right angle (less than 90°).

Right Angle: an angle that measures exactly 90°.

Obtuse Angle: an angle bigger than a right angle (more than 90° and less than 180°).

Reflex angle: an angle greater than 180° and less than 360°.

Fractions

Equivalent Fractions: fractions that look different but are equal in value (e.g. $\frac{1}{2} = \frac{2}{4} = \frac{4}{8}$).

Mixed Number: a number made from a whole number and a fraction (e.g. $1\frac{3}{4}$).

Improper Fraction: a fraction where the top number is bigger than the bottom number (e.g. $\frac{7}{4}$).

Ratio: a comparison of quantities.